HOW I BECAME
A PROPHET

HOW I BECAME
A PROPHET

IVICA PROKIĆ

Budenje d.o.o.

First U.S. edition 2014
Copyright © 2012 by Budenje d.o.o.

Published in the United States by
Awakening Within
Pahoa, Hawaii 96778

The original title in Croatian:
KAKO SAM POSTAO PROROK

First published in Croatian in 2012 by
Budenje, Ltd., Zagreb, Croatia

The CIP Number 816659 is listed in the online catalog of the University of Zagreb Library.

English edition:
Editor: Angelika Whitecliff
Copy Editor: Aliene Hughes

ISBN: 978-0-9842970-2-3

Library of Congress Control Number: 2014947380

U.S. Publisher's Website: www.Braco.net

CONTENTS

CHAPTER 3

CHAPTER 4

CHAPTER 8

THE PATH TO HAPPINESS   263

PREFACE

You have a new book before you now. Although many years have flown by with a decade and a half since our dear Ivica's passing, his nature is still here with us today. Ivica's words are deeply etched in the hearts of many who continue to remember him and celebrate his birthday with happiness and respect, and bring the gladiolus flowers he loved so very much to his grave.

In one of his wondrous prophecies, Ivica said he had been given 13 books to write in his life. He said he would let the time tell to see whether he would actually do so. And, he did. Ivica wrote all 13 books with covers in the colors of the rainbow, bringing about a special feeling:

THE CROATIAN PROPHECY—blue
THE YEAR OF HAPPINESS—yellow
THE FUTURE HAS STARTED—green
LIFE AFTER LIFE—orange
HEAVEN'S DOORS—red
JOY AND HAPPINESS IN THE TERRAIN—purple
THE PROPHECIES OF IVICA PROKIĆ—coffee with milk
GOLD PROTECTS THE EARTH—golden
THE PATH TO HAPPINESS—the color of pink cyclamen
HAPPINESS AT HOME—orange
THE GOLDEN KEY—gray
THE HEAVENS HELP US—blue-green
THE NEW BEGINNING—the white book, as whiteness, light and purity; this book is, as Ivica himself foretold, an end to some, but a true beginning to others.

Ivica considered the value of his books to be precisely because of their genuineness. For this reason they have been published as faithful records of what Ivica said, wished and thought. Hence, his message which reads:

> *My books need to be read and perused. I can justly say they are health giving, they come as a balm to a wound, and they need to be pored over anew. When you connect with my book, at that time, Spirit vivifies you and you are headed towards a brighter tomorrow. My books cannot be read and cast aside; for the protection that you will gain from them is determined by how much you love them and how much you believe in them.*

In particular, Ivica would not allow his text to be scrambled. He wished for his words to transmit his full power. For this reason they have been written down as dictated, because the spontaneous flow of his words are most valuable in his 13 books. They are the fruits of the unpredictable and inspired pronouncements of Ivica, which could not be foreseen, neither in terms of time nor content. And, as Ivica, himself, said:

> *Every book of mine has a soul. I love them immensely.*

Our wish was to consolidate Ivica's pronouncements, visions and prophecies here in one book. Thereby, an overview is given of the life and works of this extraordinary man who was, as Ivica would say, attacked and misunderstood by many and very often suffered. Respecting Ivica's will, our intention was not to scramble his words in any way, but instead, to convey them authentically in an original format. Here we hope to bring his thoughts together for clarity; both for those who once came to him and now come to Braco, as well as those who were not fortunate enough to meet Ivica.

This book contains a systemized set of Ivica's authentic texts to bring his life and work, healing mission and entire legacy to light. Simultaneously, it will serve as an explanation and introduction for easier reading of his 13 individual books. These original works carry a special magnetism and effect; one which not only we feel, but for future generations to come who shall also have the opportunity to feel and experience them, as well.

CROATIAN PUBLISHER

CHAPTER 1

A PROPHETIC PATH

―――――――――――――――――――――

AN ORDINARY MAN

I am no different from anyone else. You will see nothing different about me, and you would never notice me on the street. Maybe, only some, who have read about me in the press, could identify me. I do not have long hair, nor do I behave like a saint. I have no special or different ambitions from the rest of the world, and can say for myself that I am actually a very simple man.

One thing I wear more than other people is jewelry. You would only notice me because of my gold jewelry. This gold is the only sign that I am different from others. The amount of jewelry I wear is not to embellish myself, but because I was told to do so in a vision. I must confess that it has been very difficult for me to wear such a great quantity of gold, and it has been hard getting used to it.

But what can we do.

I was born in the country and come from a poor, working class family. Even as a child, I loved helping others.

I remember the winter of 1959, when I was nine.

We had no electricity in our village back then. It was evening and the poor neighbors were in need of cabbage brine. And, although no one had asked this of me, I took a large bowl, scooped up the brine, and took a few cabbages from my home to that family in need.

Ever since then and up to this day, wealth means nothing to me. I always turn to the poor and I am willing to help everyone.

One must be born like this. Actually, I have asked myself several times, who do I take after? I have looked over all of my family relations, and trust me; I have found no similarities with anyone. Today, I can freely say, not only to those whom I hold dearest to me, but to all people, that greed and stinginess lead to no good. One should anticipate tomorrow, but there is no need to look towards it in a material sense.

I am the last stop, the last hope towards a brighter future. You see, the light that long ago entered above the ankle joint of my left leg is the energy that is indestructible. I always say that this energy emanates straight from the Sun; that it disseminates as light does and that I am powered directly from the Sun. Thus, from here it all begins and commences.

And I live this way.

I do not wish to make anyone believe in anything that they do not wish to believe in. One should never do this. Although various people turn to me—from the begging and the unlearned, to the rich and intellectual—I do not distinguish between them. And I never will. For me, there is only one thing; we are all people. And,

I am an ordinary man who has been given to help others.

THURSDAY

One night, just as I lay down, with spirit or consciousness I travelled outside my physical body. I could see myself exiting and afterwards sitting thoughtfully in the garage.

And then I was taken into a vast, bright hall where I was carving stones. While I was working, I recognized that this was not a hall, but the church where I had been baptized as a child. I plucked weeds around this church and then noticed that there was no way out of it. Just as I had this thought, a bright light appeared. And although there were no doors, this light threw me onto the road where trucks were driving by. I asked the drivers to take me along and eventually one of them did. He took me to a city that I was familiar with, but had never been to, and I didn't know its name. The city was built along an unfamiliar body of water. Whether it was a river or a lake, I do not know. First, I was pushing in a crowd of people and then wandering the streets.

In the meantime, the city gates were shut. No one could get out except for me. By some miracle, I found myself outside the walls and nobody noticed. I wandered the suburbs until I came across a bakery with an unknown man standing at its doors.

Although we'd never seen each other before, the man turned to me and uttered the following:

> —*I see you wandering and looking for a place, but this city is closed for you. Beware; they want to destroy you! I know what it*

is you're looking for. You search for your day, but all the days have been taken!

In that instant, an unknown voice emerged:

—His day had not been taken. His day is Thursday and he has come for it.

Since then, I do not work on Thursdays. I cannot explain what it means to have been given this day, since I cannot even explain it to myself. Only for me, after this vision, I considered every Thursday as the seventh day of the week, a day of rest, like Sunday is to others. On this day, I go shopping, I rest, I celebrate it as Sunday is celebrated, and I can say that I am very happy to be the first to come for and claim this day.

THE SUN WITHIN ME

In July of 1957, I was bathing in a small river near my home village with about fifty other children. We were lying on the sand along the river. At one point, I screamed at the top of my lungs. And after crying out, I became motionless on the river's bank. Seeing this, the children ran away and I was left for dead on the sand. I later learned that the children had run off seeking help from their parents.

There was no one around me when I regained consciousness. I started shouting and calling the children. My pain was gone, with a small burn remaining above the ankle joint on my left leg. Here, in that place, I was pierced by a piece of the Sun that travelled up to my flank where it remained.

This did not bother me at all until the age of twenty-one, when I started to feel great pain. I went from one doctor to the next, until I was told in a vision that I must set off on my life's journey to a city where the crowds move like ants. Whether you believe me or not, as soon as I had a glass of water at the railway station, to my great surprise the pain stopped. From 1971 until 1986, I did not have any pain.

Imagine, from all those children, only I had a piece of the Sun burst into my leg. Now, only I carry this mark, in the sign of the cross here on my left side, and it can be seen both at night and during the day.

That piece of the Sun within me is indestructible. I am indeed in its service and shall carry it as long as my physical body endures.

This event relates to everything that later unfolded in my life.

WHO AM I?

Please, whenever you come to me at my office at Srebrnjak Street, I have always spoken about myself briefly and clearly. It is written in all my books and in the press: I am a human being like you. You then respond:

—*No, Mr. Prokić, you are more than that.*

Although I agree with you, I would never say this about myself. I let you say it.

In my life, I have gone through great miseries only to be able to say who I am today. I have always held that I am human. Today, I also say I am a man, an earthly creature, that medium working through the Spirit, through positive energy.

I can see the past, present and future. In other words, I am a man who cannot be lied to. When I say this, it really means I cannot be lied to. It is that old saying: The Earth vowed to the Heavens that all the secrets would be known.

So it is with me and with you. When you come to me, you think I don't know what you are thinking. You are not aware that it is your companion you followed at the time, who brought you to me, that spirit of the deceased from your ancestors. He has told me everything; when you cursed me, what you think of me. You laugh at me and yet say how you are my friend, a believer, but I already know everything in advance.

My dears, you see who I am. Judge for yourself. Your guardian angel tells me what you are doing, how you are doing, why you come to me, if you come out of greed, provocatively or for any other purpose.

This is it, and so you wonder, who gave me away? If you are burdened by your problems, you then say:

—*Oh God, I will go to our Ivica. Can he help us?*

Notice, you are already then helping yourself. With your faith and intuition, with your very arrival, you help yourself. So, I awaken your guide who brought you, without you understanding who actually brought you here.

You have been brought by an invisible energy.

So I say, read between the lines.

As I said, I wear gold; here is a bathing place and here is a resting place where all the doors open. And the spirit that brought you here, he tells me everything about you. So I come to know your past, present and future. I can see what you have done, why you have come, and that reason making you come to me.

This is who I am.

When I cleanse you in that great light and vivify your spirit guide, I get to know everything about you and thus help you.

I am actually a line between Good and Evil. Here with me is the last stop, when you are in great pain, praying, beseeching, calling out, crying and shouting to be helped.

Here, this is who I am.

THE SPARK OF LIFE

What I do is always for the benefit of others. I live so that whatever I myself think about, I also think of others. I could never eat and watch another starve. But I did not become like this overnight.

There must have been a spark at the time of my birth, which means that the way I am today is the way I have always been, and this is the way I will always remain.

My real name is not Ivica, but Toplica. The name speaks for itself.

Toplica relates to something warm (toplo) . . . warmth (topline), Toplica. Prokić, Proka, Prorok (prophet).

I use the name Ivica as a pseudonym.

I was born in Serbia, to my late father, Ranko Prokic, and Milosava—Mica Prokić, on August 4, 1950, in Gornja Peščanica near Aleksinac, under Mount Jastrebac. I finished my primary school in that place and lived there until the age of twenty-one.

On September 24, 1971, I came to Zagreb and stayed here. I received a Croatian citizenship and married. I am the father of two children.

I view marriage as sacred, and for me marriage is really the only consecration on this earthly world.

Enough about my personal biography.

MY FAMILY

My son Alen was a mischievous brat. Today he is already a young man, but a restless spirit. The problems I had with him I would not wish upon anyone. As his father, I had to choose his fate as such; to create his life and placed him near me, so that he would not go to the other side. At the same time, I enrolled him in school so he would mature intellectually, and I will let him stay with us until life opens its doors for him. Until then, my son will be with me until he sets off on the right path himself. He is growing stronger, more serious, and more mannered by the day, and he is less suggestible. He is able to tell black from white.

Should Alen follow in my footsteps, I would be very happy, should he not, I will let him go where he must. This means I will not create anyone's destiny, not even for my own child after he comes of age.

My wife Mara is my greatest critic. She has remained jobless since her company reorganized and she was dismissed as redundant. I saw this coming several years ago, seven years ago to be precise, before she was let go. It was not even her dream then, today a reality, to come where she belongs; that is with her husband, to follow me and be my just critic always. And, I admire her for that.

I always said she would be the last to believe.

Do not think that she has started to believe; she has not. She is only on this path to sacrifice something and once she does, then Mrs. Prokić will believe.

Then she will believe more than anyone. This is her destiny.

On the evening of November 16, 1989, while I was healing people, I suddenly had a vision of a major disaster and a great detonation near the town of Aleksinac. I heard the moans and desperate cries of people. None of those present could tell what this meant. One day later, a great accident occurred in the mines of Aleksinac.

When my wife witnessed the powers available to me, she said to me simply:

> —I did not get married to a saint, but a man. Work where you belong and stay away from bioenergy, prophecies and journalists.

She was against me helping people. She would say to me:

> —*You have your children, you have a house, you have a job, so put an end to this.*

Maybe I would have listened to her, were I able to do so. But this was not my choice.

It was not in my power.

MY FATHER

My father never loved me. Now I am forty years old and I do not want these words to hurt my father, but the truth is that during all the time of my military service in Niš, he only gave me enough money to buy two jam sandwiches. I received this much in my life from my father, and nothing more.

This vision has been published in my books and newspapers already. So here it is: Sunday, February 28, 1993.

I went to the fair and bought a car at 10 o'clock. At that time, the water tank at home ran out of water and the water pipes at my office broke.

Indeed, there are no coincidences.

We all wondered what was happening. At that time, plumbers and everyone who knew about plumbing helped so that we could find the cause.

Conversely, in the evening as my mother-in-law lay down to sleep, she saw a house with a stage within that house. Next to it was my mother and a young man of about seventeen years of age, resembling me. My father was on that stage. Then, she heard the telephone ring, but thought I would answer it. I honestly did not hear the phone. As the phone went on ringing insistently, after about 15 minutes, she finally answered it. A man from Slovenia called with the news that my father had died.

Only on the following day on March 1, 1993, did she tell me that my father had died. Even then we still did not understand the cause of the faults in the plumbing, until some people from America let us know that my father was buried on March 1st at 2:10 p.m.

With this, I want to show that the dead can affect the living, which I will later—willingly or unwillingly—have to describe.

How this all really gets in the way, I had to go through in my own skin, to be able to pass it on to you now. That is, how it works and how the underground world impacts the living.

Given that at the time Serbia and Croatia had stopped their diplomatic relations, I had to go to Slovenia so I could offer my mother financial help. She told me that she had to borrow money to bury my father. I felt a great need to go on this trip to help her. As you know, Serbia was under economic sanctions at this time. That is why I did not dare go to Niš. I told my mother we could meet in Novi Sad, where I would give her the money. And so I went on the road with my driver to do this.

We found my mother in Novi Sad, but after giving her so much money, I was afraid to let her go home by herself. So I decided to walk with her to my late father's grave. Imagine, I had already run out of gas in Svetozarev. Since this was a time of great fuel shortages, we looked for it and came to a gas station where I asked for fuel, since I travelled because of bereavement. To my great surprise, the mayor of Svetozarev Township, personally, gave me a voucher for 25 liters of fuel. During this time, police questioned my driver because the HR [Croatia] emblem with a chessboard was on the back of the car. They took our license plates, so we could resume our journey with provisional plates. Since my driver had a driver's license with a Croatian chessboard on it, a policeman wanted to penalize him saying this license was not valid here.

Several witnesses can confirm this narration. When I appeared, the policeman only looked at me, apologized sincerely and wished us a pleasant journey. He no longer debated whether the driver's license was issued in Croatia or Serbia. He only said, in amazement:

—*Sir, you actually have an effect on everyone.*

When we approached the cemetery where my father had just been buried, we made a stop in the village known as Gornja Pešćanica. My mother wanted to ask her neighbor to prepare something for us to eat when we returned from the cemetery, because my driver and I intended to head back to Zagreb immediately after.

When I got out of the car, I noticed that everyone was looking at me. To my great surprise, even the neighbor who had known me well did not recognize me. She just stared at me, as did two dozen other people who found themselves there.

Surprised, she asked my mother:

—Mica, who drove you?

My mother replied:

—Can you not recognize my son? My Toplica?

As she uttered those words, I could see everyone scattering, as if ashamed, which I did not understand at the time. We went on walking towards the cemetery. I laid five wreaths on the grave and lit candles according to the Christian tradition.

Suddenly, I heard the bird I've already described, which chitters with a rasping noise. The young man who drove me could also hear those cries. The cries were just as I had heard them in my vision. I asked my mother whether she could hear them. But neither she, nor the people present, heard the cries except for my driver and me. Afterwards, we went to the house where I was born, and several people greeted us, which really surprised me. They said:

—This is the man who dug the grave for your father.

I took the money and gave it to him. Immediately he said:

—No, no, no, there is no charge.

But I folded the money and put it in his pocket. Then I asked:

—Why are you all looking at me so strangely?

The man who had received the money replied:

—The golden man has appeared. The prophecy has come to pass.

There was a seer in these parts who made a prediction about a hundred years ago. Since I did not know anything about this before, I learned of it then. You be the judge of whether these people were lying and the future will cast its vote. I was told that this seer had visited my mother about thirty years ago, and said that the time would come when a son would fight against his father, and a brother shoot at his own brother, and the air would be polluted. At that place, a golden man would appear. When he appears, and when people recognize him, all will be put to shame. They will be ashamed because he was banished as a thief in the night.

I have laid this out for you to judge what actually happened in my village. Were these people lying?

If they have lied, let it be cast upon their honor. I am simply telling this on paper, as I have experienced it.

That journey from Zagreb to my birthplace passed as in a fairytale, if it can be called that. But, the return that lasted so long is difficult for me to describe in words. I would not wish such a journey on my worst enemy, if I had one.

My father turned evil the moment he became a servant to the underground ruler. I know he was in my way. And now, he is still trying to interfere. I have learned and actually seen how he comes from the afterlife.

How the dead can affect the living.

After I finally arrived home, I found all of my family very frightened. They did not know what kept us for so long. They became even more worried when they heard from America and

Germany that I set off on my return at 2 o'clock in the afternoon, and we had not arrived back until 2:00 p.m. the next day. The reason was a failure with the car that occurred in Hungary. You be the judge of how I felt when I saw exactly how the negative energy stopped the water flow in the engine.

Again, I went to Slovenia, and when I arrived at the border of Slovenia and Croatia, I saw my father enter a police officer at the border crossing. He blocked my way to cross the Croatian-Slovenian border. And indeed, I was not allowed to pass the border, although I had all the necessary documentation with me. Only when I managed to drive my deceased father out of the officer was I then able to enter Slovenia.

When I wanted to tell my mother that I had arrived, I dialed the number for two hours without getting through. He kept creating a fault in the connection.

Again, I saw how spiteful my father was, and how much power the negative energy commands. You see, even here I was challenged and could not get a connection. Once again, I made use of Germany, and Germany let my mother know I had arrived.

A second time I enrolled in driving school. When I went to take the exam, my father entered the examiner as before, and I ended up failing once again.

My personal driver asked:

> —*Where is your God now to help you? Every day you fall lower.*

Since I immediately saw that my late father entered my instructor,

I did not want to get him fired. So, I just passed along a small critique to him.

It happened again on Catholic Easter. My mother eagerly wanted to come to me in Zagreb, and I wished to make that possible for her. Given the political situation at the time, she had to travel through Slovenia to Ljubljana.

Imagine, an elderly woman of sixty-five years setting out on such a long journey. So, I organized for people to wait for her in Ljubljana, and my wife went along with them, whereas I stayed to see all that would happen.

I came to work in the morning, and in the presence of several witnesses told about a bus I could see driving across Hungary. As I have already said before, my son, Alen, possesses a great clairvoyant ability. People started to quiz us curiously, because what I saw, Alen saw as well, which he can confirm.

We both could see my mother sitting on a bus with other passengers. We also saw my father dressed in black, flying about the bus in anger and fury.

And although no one could see him apart from my clairvoyant son and I, we kept watching and followed him to the state border. There he suddenly entered a border official, which is when we lost sight of him.

We were told that my mother could not unite with me. My father forbade it, and so the border official sent the old woman back five times. I tried everything, but was sincerely unable to help her. I saw that the old woman had to return to Niš with unfinished business, where she remains today.

Again, my driver called me a liar and a charlatan:

—You don't really have any powers. If you had any, you would have passed the driver's test. Were you powerful, you would be able to get your mother here.

Please, the spirit of my late father had entered that young man, and drove him away from me.

Now, since that young man left, an official application was filed and my mother received a guarantee of entry into Croatia. This time, my father will not be able to prevent my mother from coming to see me. I also passed the driver's test and got my license.

Obviously my father, the late and evil spirit, cared for cutting off the people given to me, by breaking the link of the chain where it was the most sensitive. I can see that my driver will return very soon. But after he returns this time, he will no longer succumb to such evil spirits, and they will no longer affect him.

Here, I want to point out what a departed person, who entered the underground world in his lifetime, can do. He now wanders and ruins our lives. I am putting this forth for you to see how these late souls work, those who serve the underground world. They are no longer good; they are evil and dangerous. This will help you to more clearly understand why hostility and quarrels happen with those closest to us. These are the spells, as we call them, but you see; they can never be carried out without the deceased. The deceased must strictly serve the underground world, and so affect the world of the living.

Please, only yesterday you had a girlfriend, a friend, a father, a mother, those closest to you, and you were inseparable until today. Tomorrow, when you meet this person you suddenly say:

—*Hey, what's happening? Why are you looking at me so strange?*

Only yesterday, you would have given your blood, a hand or a finger for this person. Today, you feel no love, but instead hate, anger and problems.

That means that this person is constrained by your ancestor, who actually provokes these derisions to make true enemies of you.

This leads to all sorts of tricks, to various trials, quarrels and physical altercations. Actually, you are not even aware of how much hatred occurs between you, and until recently, your best friend or a blood relative.

I take my father as an example.

MY MOTHER

My mother fed the family by working the fields. As a child I would go to the fields with her, as this was the custom in the village for the children of peasants. One day, sometime in the afternoon back in 1965, I saw an old man in the woods, and he told me:

—*You won't be digging for long, and don't quarrel with your mother. She does not understand that you won't stay on to live here. In the future, you will live in a place where there are as*

18

many people as ants.

And I can say that this is Zagreb.

What was most impressionable for me was when he said the time would come when my picture would hang in the homes of people, as sacred images do. Although I believed the old man, I felt the need to tell my mother. I ran over to her and started talking in one breath. What happened to me then, how I felt, trust me, I would not wish on anyone. Not only did she beat me, she cast stones at me, yelling that I was a liar and had made something up again.

I do not know if my mother is still alive, nevertheless, she chose her own fate when she rejected and lost me. No, she is not guilty because she was blind. One can be blind with healthy eyes, as my mother was, blind in her heart. I was treated like a stepson, rejected and plied with suffering. Her daughter was everything to her, while I never felt her love.

I advise you, if you have children, when a child tells you something of that sort, don't beat and persecute him, but listen to the child. If afterwards, you feel the child should come to me, give me notice. I will talk to the child and tell you whether he is hallucinating or telling the truth.

I would not want any child to have to go through the thorny path I had to endure—an enormous discredit to a great faith.

But then, did this prophecy not come true?

And my prized mother should ask herself why you take my pictures into your homes and hang me up as a saint, bow before my picture, love and adore me, and all of this during my physical lifetime.

I can safely say that I am not a saint; I am a human being just like you. The only thing I can say for myself with certainty is that I can see the past, present and future.

MY RIGHT HAND

As I have written and talked about before, everything is predestined. Destiny commands over me, and ties me to you. This is how you began to strengthen and sprout like mushrooms after a rain. And, as a river's current, more started to come to me.

While I was still at Tuškanova Street, God held me on trial with the negative people and let me see everything and suffer. This lasted until October 11, 1993. Then came a young man of twenty-six years, named Braco, my right side, and that is when it all started.

Until this young man showed up, I had to clear my karmic debt with the underground world. What this was like for me, many well know. Some names I will not mention.

But, then he came and then it all began.

He is my right-hand side; he follows and accompanies me. Yes, you will ask me, who is he?

He is one of my reincarnated lives, the first man from the Association who came right after me; he eats what I eat, drinks what I drink. His feelings are so strong towards faith and for people; he is firm and stable on his feet. He has grown so strong that now I do not even have enough words of praise. I want him just the way he is. This young man who has never charged me a single penny and takes nothing, is directly with me.

In a vision long ago, I saw that my wife was pregnant. And though she had not been with another man, she gave birth to a child as dark as a black child. I would become the father of that child, for this is a child coming from another planet. So the time would come when I would accept him as my child.

And he came, because he had to come.

He has been appointed as the right side of myself. He is always with me, both when I sleep and when I am on the road. He is with me everywhere. He is always awake when he should be awake. I announced many years ago that he would be twenty-six years old when he comes to me.

And he appeared. Braco.

To the public, his real name has no value, for only his parents can use it to address him. For you, my right side is called Braco. And you should address him accordingly. He is in all ways similar to me; in all my feelings, he is loyal and faithful.

I could say a lot about this young man, but he, himself, says that he has now found himself, and will follow me to the grave, and over my grave, which means forever. This is what he said and this came true. No money, no wealth, nothing in this earthly world could ever separate him from me. He says he would stay even with nothing to eat, that even then he would still be here, until his death.

He says that he gives his sacrifice through the way he feels. You will see him everywhere, from Croatia to the far Australia, on all the tours, on all the journeys.

He not only eats what I eat, and drinks what I drink, he even wears gold the way I do. I will not speak about these things further now; they are for the future.

On one occasion, I told Braco that I had been on vacation, retired and that I genuinely rested in my youth. I was protected in all possible areas, for in those days such a human breakdown occurred. At that time, I was given to relax, not to worry about anything, to sleep from dawn 'til dusk, with no obligations. Then Braco said to me:

—*Oh, no. You were working. You had your family, your children; you had to feed Marijana and Alen.*

I told him the following:

—*For this I blame myself, I was human then.*

You don't understand this now, but soon you will understand. And it means that this is just a beginning compared with what is coming. You shall keep these people and the masses.

The young master did not understand, but he will understand once I explain further; I will spend the rest of my life like this and in this manner. Until my physical death, there is no rest for me, no withdrawal, no retirement; I will remain faithful to you to the end of my life. Prophets do not retire, and he is to have the same destiny. He is young today. He does not understand that the energy is with you, wherever you are, in the people, and that you guide it and speak about us.

Braco is there, directly to my right side. And you know that I've always talked about this young man who is, as you know yourself, twenty-eight years of age, who has managed to redeem and show so very much in just a year and two months. As we know, he holds a Master of Economic Sciences, he is the only child to his mother and father, and that he has arrived. As Braco himself says, the Heavens have asked this of him, and he has gracefully accepted all of it. To this day he has not committed a fault, not even as much as the measure of dirt that could fit under one fingernail. He has come with a pure soul and pure heart, to follow and accompany faithfully and trustworthily a prophet of world renown, to help him and to be close at hand everywhere and at all times.

Nowadays, many carry the symbol of the Sun with them.

This symbol has come as a bolt out of the blue. My right side came to me, and said he dreamt that he was to give me something as a gift. He wondered what it would be, what could he reward me with? After putting a lot of thought into it, he then decided to present me with a symbol of the Sun. Without my permission, he went to a jeweler and had an imprint made according to the symbol from a book of mine, crafted in gold.

Afterwards he came to me and said:

> —*Mister Prokić, I do not know whether my decision is right or wrong, but I consider you my great teacher and father. The only thing I want is to be with you, if you allow it. In addition, I wish to give you this beloved symbol so you may carry it with you.*

I looked at the young man and asked:

—*Where did you get the money to buy me this?*

To my great criticism, he answered that the symbol he gave to me was paid for with his own money, which was not stolen, but earned honestly and decently. What else could I do but use my clairvoyance to find out what this young man was offering me. The inner Voice said:

—*Accept this young man's gift, and for his birthday buy him a gold symbol and gold chain.*

Then, I told him:

—*I will accept the gift under the condition that I do the same in return, in equal measure.*

He agreed, and I did so. I also told him the following:

—*Son, do not brandish your money, if you understand me. All you have, give to your father, so my hands are clean. I am an honest man; you can stay with me under the condition that you don't wave your money about. I want you under these conditions. Forget the money where it is.*

And so the young man agreed and since then, the masses have followed this symbol and people wear it. How much it helps them, and how much it helps you is for you to determine. I do not want to make a judgment on these matters; you are the ones who judge.

Braco speaks:

—I had to be this way. Long ago, even as a child, I was different from other children. I asked myself whether I really knew myself enough; am I really this person or someone else.

I am an only child of a wealthy and well-situated family. Everything I could wish for I would receive from my parents. I was not short of anything, from fast and luxurious cars to all the rest. By the time I was twenty-six, I had finished studying and completed all the schooling that life had dictated to that point, so I then founded my own company. Nonetheless, I would always wander, looking for something. Simply, there was something stronger in me. Then in my twenty-sixth year, my wandering came to an end the moment I walked through the door to Ivica Prokić.

Ever since, we are never separated.

I rejected the material world and became devoted to the spiritual. That is why I am here in this place. Nothing can separate me, and nothing can sway me away from this area.

ON A PROPHETIC PATH

On Friday, September 19, 1989, I returned home from work and lay down to rest. It was about 4:00 in the afternoon. I suddenly saw a door opening, which had never existed in the room before. Then a great bright light appeared that covered me and propelled me into the sky. It carried me all the way to a great castle, whose appearance is absolutely impossible to describe.

This can only be seen in a dream. It was constructed entirely of gold, yet transparent, as if made of glass. In it there were pillars, forty-one in number. On top of the pillars was a crown, five times five meters in size and 170 centimeters in height. The crown was adorned with spires.

As I was observing it, one of the spires spoke:

> —*My son, you have come. There are 39 steps behind you.* (It was the number of my years at the time.) *Now you only need to pass another two steps and you will be with me.*

I asked, wondering:

> —*But who am I? Am I not the son of Ranko Prokić?*

The crown replied:

> —*I am your spiritual father.*

After that, the light returned me back home.

I saw myself lying down, but to enter my physical body, I had to go through the same door I exited. Then, joining the body brought me great sweetness and pleasure. Connecting my spirit and physical body was an exceptional enjoyment. I must stress that I felt this sweetness flow for three days: through me, and throughout my body that sweet, sweet energy constantly flowed.

Time and again, I say there are no coincidences.

Everyone has his own path. The path I am treading is destined.

This is one great prophetic path.

CHAPTER 2

A GAZE INTO THE FUTURE

A CANDLE'S FLAME

People often ask me why a candle is burning while I am prophesying. You see, everything that happens in a human life is visible on their candle of life. If an individual gains weight, his candle thickens at this site beforehand, signifying the extra kilograms.

When someone experiences a car accident or something similar, his candle of life breaks first. Even once broken, it continues to burn for as long as the individual is destined to live. Once the candle's flame goes out, no life remains in the physical body. All such candles of life are white in color, and are just as tall as the human adult's height in life.

An entire human life is programmed into these candles. In the same moment when a baby is born, a candle of life is lit for that newborn. This is a candle that burns for as long as he lives. Since our life is assigned to each of us in advance, the candles are of various sizes and thicknesses.

Likewise, candles are lit in heaven for each existing country in the world. Individual countries last as long as their candle's burn. One can see many things in the flame, which is why I cast the light of the candle onto a mirror.

As the candle is burning, I receive the spark in the flame. In that moment when a person wishes to talk to me, he sits across from me and the light of his eyes reflects in the flame. The flame carries me to the spark of life and I begin to see the past, present and future of that person.

I cannot see everyone's future. There are people whose light does not reflect in mine at all, and I cannot tell them anything. Actually I can, but I am spared from them, because they belong to the underground world. I do not admit such people for if I did, I would become nervous and I would have to bluff. That is why I resolve this by rejecting them. At the time when I drive such a person out, I have power over them, but they only need to return and say the following words:

—*Please, admit me.*

At that moment, I would admit the person and work with them in the same manner that I work with all the rest.

It is worth knowing that one comes to me without an announcement, without an appointment, without any kind of prior notice. I am available for all people, in a good temperament, in the measure that I have been given.

If you ask me how many people I can receive in a single day, I would say that it is between 150 and 200. However, without any fatigue, just as when I came to work, I leave feeling just as fresh. This has always been surprising to my visitors and friends.

I am always dynamic and full of energy at any time of day or night. I never get up feeling irritable, moody or angry.

I am unable to be like this and I do not know myself as such.

SPHERE IN HAND

The visions can hold the key to our future, to be seen and looked into, and when interpreted well, the key is in our hands.

Visions come to me when I want to foretell the future of a person. It is sufficient for me to know their full name and date of birth to tell them about what once was, what is now and what will happen in their future, even though I have never seen them before in my life and literally know nothing about them.

However, I cannot describe future events to everyone. I cannot tell them to individuals who are exceptionally closed, and those who are unknowingly filled with the negative energy of the underground world. When I see them, nothing speaks from within me.

It was about 1:00 p.m. when I was strolling with my wife down Zvonimir Street, and I happened to look up at the sky. I saw a huge clock hovering above the street, actually a huge star in the shape of a clock, with its hands showing 12:55. I asked my wife:

—*Do you see this?*

—*What?*

She replied with a counter question, and it was clear to me that she could not see what I saw.

Later while on the bus, I constantly looked up at the huge star that looked like a clock, which no one could see except for me. I saw it in the evening too, and it was still in front of my house the next morning.

That morning as I was healing people, every now and then, I would go to the balcony and observe this star that was following me. I tried finding out from those being treated whether they could see it or not.

Here something really extraordinary happened. All those present, everyone there, saw the star, too!

However, the next day, no one except for me could see it. I was looking at it and was able to see it regardless of whether my eyes were open or closed. The star was present even in the following days. I was constantly observing it.

Then on July 6th, at around 10:00 p.m., as I was observing the star from my room, I suddenly saw a great golden tree within it. My mother walked around the tree, watering it. I am sure I would have been told much more if one of the neighbors hadn't barged into the room at that very moment, shaking me and diverting my attention from what I was seeing in the star. When he left and the insignificant conversation was over, I tried to make out something in the star again, but with my physical eyes open, I could not.

A day later, at the same time and in the same place, I saw with my physical eyes that star which the others could not see.

But this time, I saw that I was in it, holding a sphere in my hand.

THE MIRROR TELLS THE FUTURE

For now, I look into the future through my old mirror. Here I see the past, present and future. It is the oldest little mirror.

My people have asked me:

—*But what if someone steals it from you?*

—*That's their business. Even if they steal it, it will not tell them anything.*

The future is always as one rhythm, flowing between Good and Evil. There is always a little bit of sugar and a little bit of wormwood, and the human life follows in this way.

The future comes after each morning, it comes in the evening; after the day comes the night, and after every night comes the day.

And so it is to a better tomorrow.

If a person comes and I tell him to be on the watch for various things, he is then aware of this and only has to look a little bit, when I say to look a little bit, at tomorrow, so he will indeed cast aside that injustice.

When I say, do not get married at a particular time, wait until before or after, this is the near future.

This is our future.

Just as I look into the future of a country, I look into the future of a person. As to how I look into the entire future, my dears, I leaf through and read mankind's books of life.

I am happy to watch your future and our future. Nostradamus used to make predictions using a mirror as I do today. And now, I am served by using his same old mirror.

By some strange wonder, I had never even heard of the existence of Nostradamus, until I was told about him by a journalist, who laughingly said to me, Nostradamus was the one and only prophet.

Again, I knew nothing.

You can imagine, I, who had hardly read anything before, did not know this. I did not like to read or it simply did not interest me. And how was I supposed to know all of this existed if there was not someone to tell me about it.

Naturally, the mirror for both of us is only a means, as are all other items that are used exclusively for attaining better concentration during divination.

The most common are reading coffee grounds, beans, reading destinies from the stars, a palm, lead in water, embers in water and reflecting on a white cloth.

I do not know if anyone has worked with the mirror besides Nostradamus and me. But, I am a man who looks into the flame, casting it to the mirror for me to tell the future.

In the beginning, I did not work with the mirror. One night, as I was lying in bed, the image of a bearded old man appeared to me, and said:

—Look under your pillow and take what you find. In it is all that people need!

I awoke startled and anxious hearing those words, and I really did look under my pillow. There lay an old mirror, which I now use today for my predictions, because in it I see all the events that will happen.

Since having the mirror, I see future events and the answers in it, and not only in my visions.

So I became a prophet with the mirror.

DESTINY HAS LEFT THE DOOR AJAR

A long time ago, through my books and in the press, I made it known that I saw myself surrounded by a mass of people. Amongst them, at my side, was the young man I have been announcing.

That young man was sitting on my right side, and I had on a white shirt and dark trousers, that is dark-blue trousers. In addition, one pair of shoes was completely finished, while the other pair had not yet been prepared for use; it was still in the process of creation.

You can imagine how I felt then, at that time when everyone

made fun of me, and I can safely say that I also thought that I had gone crazy as well.

But today, for you and for me, this prophecy has also come true. Please understand, one pair of shoes was finished, like the white shirt. The other pair of shoes was still being prepared, and today this is experienced and seen in the following way:

This young man sitting on my right represents the second pair of shoes that are still not ready for spiritual binding. His time is coming; his path of life will open.

Destiny has opened the door for him, so in the times to come, we shall be announcing him and you will see him in this way, as I have foreseen.

HEAVEN'S DOORS

Some time ago, back about ten or twelve years, I arrived on the banks of the Sava River in the vicinity of Zagreb, where I saw a wall. Please note that this is a vision, which I will fully lay out for you, just as it all happened. Suddenly, I saw a woman standing there with large forks. They were like the iron pitchforks that farmers use in their fields to collect hay. She held both forks in her hands, and waved them to and fro, trying to stab my child. She was attempting to stab my son, Alen, directly in the heart.

I was so terrified that I started to scream. It was completely shocking because I did not know why she wanted to stab my child. Then, on the other side, I saw and recognized her son. I can freely say that this woman was deceased at the time, and I was extremely surprised. So, I screamed and begged her son to stop his mother from destroying my child.

I really did not understand the message. I thought I was hallucinating or dreaming. Exactly then, it was announced that the doors between Good and Evil, namely Heaven's doors, were located here.

A few days after that vision, I went for a walk and quite accidentally came to the very same place.

Who drew me there, I would ask you.

What is this energy that brings you to your Ivica Prokić?

Thus, an invisible energy took me to the place where I saw that woman attacking my child. When I got there, I recognized that this was the place where it happened, and saw some old car on a hill. A little further on, I saw a man bathing in a natural pool, or some kind of pond. I asked him why he was bathing naked, and he coldly replied that he lived there.

—*How long have you been living here?* I asked him curiously.

—*I used to have a hut but they demolished it, so I moved into this old car.* He responded.

—*What is your name?* I asked further.

—*Đuro.* The poor man replied.

Afterwards, as I was returning home, something stirred in me, so I started taking food and clothing to give to that man, Đuro. After a few years, I started talking about this amongst my neighbors. They said they knew of him, he was Đuro, *The Hermit*. I asked one neighbor if he would like to give something to him and he agreed. It was about 10 o'clock at night during the winter, with snow, and we set off to see Đuro. We brought him all sorts of things to eat

Then I realized one day I would have to build him a house.

I asked myself:

—*But come on, Ivica, how could you build Đuro a house?*

I had no money, so I mentioned this idea to my neighbor, who smiled and said I should go from house to house and ask the other neighbors for charity to build him a home. This neighbor of mine was well situated and had a lot more money than I did, but had no children. Yet, he simply started to ignore and ridicule me.

My illusions then came to an end.

Again, I was obstructed at this time by these tyrants. I went on giving whenever I had something—food, or some clothes. I would also give him money or cigarettes. For almost a year, they mocked this, at my expense.

They asked:

—*You fool, how are you going to build Đuro a house?*

They would keep ridiculing me, while I retreated into myself. So, I waited for a divine sign. I waited for it until just a few days ago.

Yes, you will ask me how I could know, one hundred percent, that

Đuro was guarding Heaven's doors?

Yes, he guards them. But Đuro does not know what he is guarding. I will recount this later for you and try to explain who this man is.

Just as my son, who was eleven and a half years old at the time, knew where his dad constantly brought food, so did Đuro learn that he was my child. The youngster also started to bring food without my knowledge. He would often say that he was not hungry; that he had to take Đuro food so he could eat.

He would always say:

> —*Mom, give this to me without telling dad. If dad finds out, he won't take food to him. Đuro is hungry; I can't stand that he has nothing to eat.*

Then, once, my son brought food to Đuro and he felt like bathing in the pond with the other children. However, of all the children, the accident I saw in my vision was to happen to him.

Consequently, my child came very close—as the doctors' say, an inch away from dying. It was exactly as I saw it. I stress that the child did not know that danger was lurking, and he went where he should not have gone.

And so it all began.

I was very angry with the boy for his disobedience, until I heard a Voice that said to me:

> —*Ivica, dear, the boy wanted to open the doors, but before you*

came! He, too, has the gift of clairvoyance, and Marijana has your kindness. He is a child just trying to enter the doors of Heaven. Given the woman with the forks was standing there, everything has ended well.

She was supposed to stab him, but as you can see, your kindness and quick intervention saved the child.

This is how I came to know that the doors of Heaven were located here.

I owe a detailed explanation. First, I want to say that Evil is so far away from, and yet so close to, Good. Evil and Good are always side by side. On one side there is Paradise, and on the other, Hell. That is why the doors of Heaven are set. The guards are good on one side, but evil on the other.

I then proceeded to ask:

—Well, who actually is Đuro?

The voice said to me:

—You will see. You promised to make him a house and you will do so one day, when the time comes. He will not settle for this, he will be with that woman at the time, Ivica, and she will then be within him. But do not be discouraged; immediately thereafter, on the following day you will have an immense and great marriage. You will release your karmic debt, and he will begin to bathe in alcohol, so let him stay where he belongs.

So, on January 26, 1995, only two days ago, I went with my people to make Đuro a place of residence, a home of wooden planks.

Please, we started in the morning and in just a few hours a dwelling sprang up from the turf, which you can see on the videotapes. Thinking that he would settle there, we gave Đuro the keys.

In the evening of January 27, 1995, when we went back to him, we found Đuro lying in that old car again, like a dog by the fire. We recorded all of this. He even spat at us. This was no longer the Đuro we used to know.

He was drunk and that damned spirit of the woman spoke through his mouth. Instead of thanking us, he offered ridicule, saying it was better to live in the car than in that shack we had built him.

Please, I will not give away the place where this hermit lives, because his life is there in that car. He has been guarding the doors, until a person appeared who is already working with me and who now faithfully protects the key to the doors.

Đuro gave in to alcoholism and is now in the underground world, where he belongs. Until recently, angels kept him warm, and today angels are replaced by alcohol. How long the alcohol will keep him warm, time will tell.

Last night, when I was directly at the doors of Heaven, I saw that the key was already in the hands of my man; happily and with my head up, I went back towards Srebrnjak. So, God immediately brought a man from the Association, and handed him the key to Heaven's doors.

The key is in the hands of my man. I am not going to name him, so that the key will not be of any harm to him.

39

He will protect it and be opening the doors to Heaven.

ON SREBRNJAK 1

From the doors to Heaven, I came directly to Srebrnjak 1. Both today and yesterday, as in the future, multitudes of people will pass here.

A whole river of living people come.

I saw all of this twelve years ago. At that time, I spoke of receiving the message that I would one day be married. For the miracle of it, I did not understand the message at the time, but the message was that I would be married with Spirit.

That is what I experienced.

We know that I made my way through a difficult path, in the path of life. Long ago, I came to Šubiceva Street, to Mira, where I stayed for exactly two and a half months. From Šubiceva, we came to Tuškanova Street, where the word spread about a man who allegedly helps. They placed me in the same category as those fortunetelling hags, witches and sorceresses.

So I had to endure this thorn filled path to get to what we have now. I stayed there a full 32 months.

Fateful intuition, the Voice, led me to Srebrnjak 1, where I stayed for 23 months into the New Year of 1995.

The Voice also said not to worry about the rent, it must happen this way. And I was told that I would write books. But, soon after the New Year I would receive a new message: where to go next, where to move and where to settle.

Arriving at Srebrnjak, I again had a great vision: At the doors, which were closed at that time, both to me and you, stands that woman once again, but this time Rada will not let her pass and stubbornly explains something to her. I exclaimed:

—*Let her come to me, Rada, to see what she wants.*

I believe that you understand what I am saying. Rada is my cook and my very faithful person. A Cross appeared on the doors, a huge Cross plastered with wallpaper. Please, great light in the form of a drill started to spin and disintegrate that Cross. All of a sudden the doors opened and a Voice told me:

—*Here, this is ours, we have won. The Heavenly doors are finally opened. The key came directly to one of my people.*

Then, we quickly called the owner and asked him if he would be willing to sell us the apartment. The owner could hardly wait to hear this and said:

—*Come, children, Mr. Ivica, the apartment is yours.*

Thus, on January 3, 1995, we entered into a new beginning.

In record time, we completely rearranged the old into the new. In one month it is finished, the house where we will spend our time, which leads us into a brighter tomorrow. This is the house where the unhappy, sick, ugly, sad, blind, and the beautiful will peacefully come, and I will admit them all with equal measure.

I never ask anyone who he or she is.

At these doors, everyone is always welcome. I have never turned anyone down, and I will admit everyone, even if for some reason, I am not in the mood for talking.

At Srebrnjak, something new begins. It is a new beginning, with new people, new times, and a new civilization. In a short while, I see such masses coming that I do not know how and in what way we will be able to admit them.

WHY PEOPLE COME TO ME

Some come from wantonness, some to deceive God, some to mock, some to see the prophet, some to be helped, but there are few who genuinely believe. People think that I do not see this. Well, they are half asleep.

But when they wake up and when all is realized, they will repent.

Those who believe will be blessed, those who do not believe, let them be judged. I never call myself the Almighty, I do not slander anyone, and I am doing all of this because I was given the ability to do so. I have never worn Gold to act like some kind of a rich man. When someone calls me names, saying I wear jewelry like a gypsy in Gold, and that I am a rich man, I would give anything to switch places, so that I may follow him and not have it be the reverse. Very few of those born can endure all of this, to help from dawn until dusk, day after day, without asking the cost of it all.

I have always maintained that he who wishes to reward me may leave only as much as he can, on the table where I work.

Just that much and no more.

In the introduction, I said why people come to me. But, my dears, you know that in the beginning when they come, everything begins to unfold for them and flow like water. Afterwards, they forget this, so they start to mock and laugh at me, then slander, until something stops again. That is when they return, asking for help, and this is how it continually goes on and on.

I can say that there are few of those who truly believe.

There are some, but this is only just a beginning.

In a short while, I see a tremendously large number headed towards belief, because as I say, they are brought by an invisible energy. That is, they are led to the light, which intensifies through my Gold in that light. Their ancestors see this light, and they simply enter the spirit of that person, trying to redeem themselves through you, their relative. Your ancestors bring you, so that they may be redeemed, as well as you.

When the negative energy sees that your matters are improving, it begins its orgies to plot and turn you away from your Ivica Prokić. Then you start to think negatively about him.

In the beginning we would not even have known each other. You would come, I would tell you the reason for your arrival, and identify your problems. I would delve into your life and your life problems. You would be impressed, joyful and happy.

Suddenly, something gets in the way and you slander me the next day.

Why? You do not know, but I do. You were weak.

You were used in some common way and you simply started to allow yourself to be taken in by this mood; you did not ask yourself how much you had gained from coming and how much you were helped by this man.

So then you start off slandering.

In such moments, the negative energy is very strong.

You grow stronger by slandering, ridiculing and belittling. And, it goes so far that you no longer have the courage or the heart to reappear at my doorstep, even though you may have regained your senses. You no longer have the courage to come here, because you know that I know about your prior slandering and ridicule. I am clairvoyant and you are aware of it. That is why you start to look for other people, with whom you go and bargain, like you are shopping at the market.

Then you begin to publicly admit that you have been to Ivica Prokić, and that he helped you, but for some unknown reason, you are unable to go back to him. At that time, you are lying to yourself; observe how you drag yourself even deeper into the underground world. Some of you lie about paying me and those listening to you believe you. In this way, you place a barrier so that you cannot go back to the place where you once were.

This is it, my dears, why you are coming and why you are leaving work unfinished. I will illustrate a case. A woman came to me, so shy and noble, that I called her a queen. At that time, I was tested along with her. The lady actually considered herself to be a queen. I saw and had to taste it myself, as well as all the others. From one day to the next, she became a medium. She started imitating me and play-acted the role of Ivica Prokić.

All until something happened, on January 8, 1995 in KriŽevci.

Although I was invited, the host did not expect me. I asked the mirror, as I always do, how and in what way I should go there.

The mirror told me:

> —*You may go, but this time, don't take Braco along, take Pero. And you can go freely. The path is open to you. On this path you will see everything.*

On January 8, 1995, at 10:30 in the morning, I arrived at a family house in KriŽevci. Carefully follow what happened to me, because I would not wish this on my worst enemy. When I arrived, the host greeted me with great surprise. He tried to pretend, but I went into the house and saw that he was prepared to host some kind of great performance that was already imitating Ivica Prokić.

Two tables were formally prepared for the guests. When I entered, they did not even know where to seat me. I was situated some place on the side, since I saw "the queen" was supposed to sit at the head of the table. Please, I sat down humbly. Believe me, what I saw at the time was urging me to turn around and return home, but I had to remain as an ordinary man and go through this humiliation.

In about 5 minutes, the calls and cries announced that "the queen" had arrived. People were delighted, rejoicing and crying out with glee. She entered with self-importance, playing Mr. Prokić, but when she saw me, she was extremely surprised. I was unwelcome in their company. Because I was present, they had no freedom. I wanted to end it all, but the Voice said:

—*No. Stay a little longer.*

At the time, I forgot that Braco was not beside me, but Pero instead. Pero had only been with me for a month. The young man did not understand any of this. God forbid, if Braco had been there he would have smashed everything in the house. So, we just looked on as observers and not guests. I drank the coffee but did not eat. There was no lunch for me. Naturally, "the queen" had her throne, and I, as a beggar had to leave because I was not welcome.

This lasted only on that day and never again.

So please, do not do this. And when I name you, know that you are being tested. You have to follow and accompany faithfully, because there is one Sun and I get my energy from it. It can burn you when you least expect it.

So please, do not imitate me. You won't do it for long! I cannot be decoded. Who I am, you shall see. Why I have come, you will know.

WHY DO SOME MALIGN ME?

I know that as you read and re-read me, you will say: *My God, are there really such people that slander him?!*

You would be surprised, but there are indeed those who slander me.

Yes, there are people who have never seen me, but call me the Antichrist. They say I belong to some sect, that I am a charlatan, a thief, who puts out a pot for people to throw their money and gold into, and that I bring people in just to hijack their gold.

That is slandering.

They wonder what sort of a saint I am when I swear.

Yes, what sort of a saint am I, when you see that I have never called myself a saint. How can I be a saint when I am the father of two children, a man like you?!

When I say I am a prophet, there is no reason to slander me; but as we can see, they do.

Why do they malign me?

I will try to explain how people have slandered my many years of work. Here, I first want to say that I will not name anyone. It is not that I am afraid; I will not out of courtesy.

If they malign me, I will not malign them. It has always been this way, and it will continue to be so.

I recently said that an Angel tells me everything, that I am a direct guide from the Sun, that I am full of enthusiasm and zeal, that I do all of this honestly, that I follow the path of justice, the path of love, that I was born into Christianity and that I am a child of Jesus Christ, that I am God's chosen person, that I am not some kind of crude dogmatist, but simply the most natural person, as natural as can be.

But I will not go into my great abilities.

When a person comes to me, I first tell him all about himself.

At that time, he begins to trust me. As I just said, he starts elevating me to the Heavens. And for him, I become God. But, when he is taken to think that he, himself, managed to solve those previous problems, the underground world enters this thoughts and he begins to study me.

When you come to this point, you cannot continue. All slander and speaking ill of me stems from this great malice and jealousy.

And, so it goes on.

Some fear I might ruin them, some fear I might jeopardize their job, some fear that if I shine, they will disappear.

And, this is the way it goes on.

Those practicing black magic fear me as the devil fears incense. Others desire to get rich overnight; I cannot provide this for them, since I live a modest life. These are the slanderers. Some become jealous because the media constantly monitors me, and some women get jealous and slander me because they cannot become my mistress. In addition, they come because they allegedly have some difficulties and problems, but in fact they greatly desire to seduce me. Men, with their wives, become jealous because their wives keep coming to me and so they fear that I might take them over. Please, I am neither one, nor the other, or anything of this kind. I have my own family. I have not come here to create anyone's destiny.

If I have not helped, I have definitely not hindered.

To everyone, I offer love, joy, prosperity and happiness. People simply want something, without knowing what they want. First they come seeking help. When they see that help arrives, they latch onto the material. When they have gained materially, they want more. They would like to drive a Mercedes or similar cars. People will be people. When they see they cannot have it all, they begin to slander me, and say that I did not help them. Until recently, they would glorify me; now suddenly, they slander me.

This is the human side.

Yes, you will ask who actually praises me the most?

Please understand, everyone comes to me with his or her own goal and reason. Some come to get rich, some from wantonness, some to be helped with an illness, but some come to follow and walk along a great path.

For now, I can freely say that there are a few of those who believe. They believe and they will never slander me. Even in their greatest pain, they would not reject me. They will go through their karmic journey, a life's journey, and will be helped.

This is for certain.

I say this from personal experience.

I have had many different problems and hardships. When I

thought there was no way out, suddenly someone would help me. And again, I would rise up on my own two feet.

But why do so many come, and why do I go through so much?

It is because I give a lot and charge nothing for it; this is my greatest virtue and my greatest strength.

I would love to see anyone stand up and say I robbed or cheated them, or ever falsely promised anything to anyone. I am always looking to help. But I have never said; it is over now, I have helped you.

Instead, I say: Go and sing, be happy and rejoice.

Please understand, what comes after this is one great awakening, one great temptation. This is how a brighter tomorrow is made.

Those who believe do not slander me. Only those who want a lot, and give a little, do it, those who come expressly on a mission, to spitefully harm or test both me, as well as you.

I will give you an example, one case.

One of my followers glorified me such as our former "queen", and also attempted to emulate me. Please, such low blows are not even worth mentioning. These are the people who genuinely do not know themselves, who do not know what they are doing, and are too overconfident. I immediately knew that this woman would slander us.

And, it did indeed happen.

This person slammed us and in a short time realized what she had done, and that she was powerless. She got a slap in the face by God, and came back to tell us all about it. Note that she comes here today, but we do not say anything, we act as if nothing has happened. She pays for her sins herself.

So please, to badmouth today is to bootlick tomorrow. Do not do it.

If you slander us, do not come any longer. We will accept you, but you will no longer sit at the place where you sat yesterday. I have said, if you repent for doing something unconsciously, you may receive forgiveness, but for doing it consciously, repentance is useless.

Humankind has been created to work and so create the future. Therefore, you cannot simply go out on the street and ask God to help you, since even a roast chicken and bread require you to work. So it is with me. They come and it's free.

But one cannot live off praise; neither can I.

So this means that if I have helped someone, he can come and say, sir, you have helped me and I wish to leave something. This is a different matter.

But, here you go, I get slandering as pay. That has been my payment thus far.

I know I spoke long ago, saying that if I had a kilogram [35 ounces] of gold, I would be a direct guide with the Sun. Then, because of the shame, I did not even believe myself. It was really impossible the amount of mockery I received at the time. I spoke then as I speak to you now.

They ridiculed me, and said:

> —*You scab, who would ever give you a kilo of gold, where would you hang it? It's a lie.*

Then, is it a lie when you see me in gold, and when you say that you don't know me any other way, and that I would be unusual without this gold?

Are these your words? Find out for yourself.

Those that mocked me, please, I feel sorry for them today. I will be saying in a short while that I am sorry for you as well, but by then, I will not be able to help you.

Please, all I say happens, so I advise you, do not put a barrier on your own path.

STRENGTH, HELP ME

All my astral journeys and visions are accomplished with the help of my Spirit guide or Strength.

He is faceless to me. When he lifts me and takes me high up to see what will be, I always feel sorry for using him for these purposes.

This Strength does not have any special appearance, but whenever I think of it and call it to mind, it comes.

It has never betrayed me so far. I just call:

—*Strength, help me!* And I immediately fly.

As I have said, I not only see in the mirror, but also without the mirror when I am not at rest. When I cannot go on an astral journey, then I call on the great mirror to work through it, but I am not always allowed to see through it. I do this when I find myself in any kind of unclear area. Then, when I call on the great mirror the Heavens reveal what I need to know. I receive everything through the chained path. I see everything, but I do not do this always, only when it is absolutely necessary.

I must say, you see me closing my eyes several times, looking to see something. I do this to find a missing person, when I bring something unclear into its primal position.

But beforehand, I call and pray:

—*Strength, can you see this man; tell me about him, so we may see and know everything, tell me all about him.*

After repeating this prayer twice, I arrive precisely at the place where the incident occurred. As I said, it is from where a human being begins, the journey he takes, and how he returns to this place, from where he started.

So, this is how I do everything, when I close my eyes, and utter these words, I set off on a journey, to see the event. Whether a person is dead or alive is revealed to me. When I see that someone is deceased, I look at the person seeking the missing person, assess well and ask the mirror.

In very few cases do I say what really happened to that person, and if they are dead or alive. When I see that someone is deceased, I usually say there is a big fog in front of me and apologize because I cannot see clearly. I kindly send them out, and sometimes an individual realizes that I did not directly say what really happened to the missing person for a reason.

So, please, after all those people are examined, after all this good work, you must understand that I find it the hardest when I have to speak about something as sad as this.

I do not like sad news and will not communicate it.

I am the happiest when I am able to speak to people only about the nicer matters, and would always want it to be this way.

This again is my manner of working.

One can see everything in the mirror; realize that the mirror never lies. It is so powerful that even cameramen have tried filming the mirror, to capture what is actually happening.

They were able to record some images in the mirror that were very unclear, but we will leave this for science to one day assess.

This means that all can be seen. Some have tried to catch a glimpse of something in my magic mirror, but then smilingly tell me that all they see is their own reflection.

To this I return the smile and say:

—*What can I do, when you cannot see what I can see.*

There is something else I wish to communicate about clairvoyance. Every day, I am visited by more and more new people.

Actually, my mirror.

But, are you not my mirror?

For you are the mouths that carry me. Do I not speak through your mouth?

You be the judge of this.

CHAPTER 3

THE PROPHECIES

―――――――――――――――――

THE AWAKENING

I know that it troubles you but I will always keep you at a distance from me, because I know the key and the path to all of which I speak.

Judgment day is coming and the day of the new civilization, of the new baptism. That day, as I have said, is not far off and everyone will see and feel it. When the great awakening occurs, there will be no more wars. Then, all the weapons and arms will go silent and humanity will resume its true path: the path of the Sun, the path of God and the path of Love.

But, people have been asleep for exactly two thousand years.

Yes, you will ask me, how are we alive yet not awake?

Well then, please, why do we kill and devour each other?

The Divine does not grant us this. Why is there so much sorrow, suffering and pain cast over man? It is because negative energy has the power, and power is money.

Yes, you will ask me, how can it be money?

Please, everything revolves around money; money buys weapons— to kill humankind. Please, why it does this, you will decide for yourself.

That day is not far away, we shall all see it, some will repent, but those who have believed will be saved. These are the prophecies of the new civilization. Maybe some will ridicule me, and I know some will make fun. Some will even be terrified of me, but there will be those who will believe me. I am not speaking this; Heaven is speaking it.

Please, you be the judge of whether I am telling the truth or whether this is my crazy imagination. I do not daydream, but if someone attributes that to me, he will repent.

Mankind has been sleeping for the past two thousand years. And now when I say that the day is not far off, and that we shall all see it, please, this is the awakening, when mankind will wake up.

Please, visualize yourself asleep, are you living now? No, because one could dream he was back in time—through Spirit—two thousand years ago when we were free. But this dream is brief, and it is only valid for the Spirit, because man is a material, corporeal being.

Instilled with the Spirit of God, man actually sleeps. This is why during this time there have been so many wars, and why it is said that something has gone missing. Something man could never know.

What was Atlantis, people wonder to themselves.

Atlantis is one part of humanity that has been transported and relocated to a safe place; whereby, one part of mankind sleeps—and the other lives. Atlantis is a continent, which at that time simply disappeared. It was taken, transferred, and when we shortly reunite with our brothers and sisters, we shall see what they have gained and what we have lost.

Then, you will understand and comprehend that we have been asleep for two thousand years, even for the time of the awakening. The awakening will occur when the people appear from Atlantis.

But someone has already arrived, that I can freely announce.

HOW NOSTRADAMUS SAW ME

On September 15, 1990, as I was resting in bed, at one point I looked out the window and in that instant, I went on an astral journey.

I was taken to the home of my birth. Through the window of that house, I saw the same scene that I had watched through the window of my own house. My father was passing by, and behind him walked my cheerful and smiling late grandfather, and behind the two of them was a bearded man. He introduced himself as Nostradamus. Who he was and what he did, I did not know, even his name meant nothing to me. Everything would be explained to me two years later.

Behind him passed another ten strangers who brought me a completely unfamiliar machine with big gears like those of an enormous clock.

The man with the beard said:

> —*This, son, I give to you. I have come to this point, but you will use it from now on, for the next 850 human years.*
>
> *Remember, my name is Nostradamus!*

There, the vision ceased. I returned to my physical body and awoke shivering. I had to drink a glass of sugared water to calm myself down.

I repeat that the name Nostradamus meant nothing whatsoever to me at the time, and I only came to know later that he is one of the most famous prophets in human history.

All the prophecies, or at least in specific parts, are given using symbols. To interpret and come to an understanding of the facts about the future through these symbols, a key is needed. This key is not always easy to find.

For example, the search for the right key for some of Nostradamus's quatrains is still ongoing. Therefore, it is not surprising that so many versions and attempts of interpretation are given for his complex symbols and metaphors.

Nostradamus, as many others, used only words to describe the images he saw of the future. However, in these descriptions, sometimes factual details are missing, those core details that would finally help to untangle the intricate bobbin.

The same problems occur with my prophecies.

Thus, I am subjected to ridicule, and go uncomprehended.

However, we will let time heal all wounds, and people who see can freely talk about the past, present and future.

Long ago, I often spoke about the old man, and described everything in my books, yet I did not realize who I was describing. At the time, I did not know, nor had I heard anything about the man named Nostradamus. This great and famous name of a phenomenal leader and teacher, doctor, astrologer and God's messenger, who lived 500 years ago. He predicted all of this ...

And Nostradamus said:

—*From the aquatic triplicity there is born a man.*

Please. I am Christian, and I was born during the time of water, in the sign of the Sun. This is the code if you did not know. This means I was born in triplicity.

And Nostradamus said:

—*And Thursday will be his celebrated day.*

So, am I not celebrating Thursday? I am the first man in the world to be given an unclaimed day, the day of Thursday.

And Nostradamus said:

—*When Spirit appertains and grows strong ... bringing trouble to the East.*

I have already said, the conception lies with the three Cross-Mountains: Belgrade, Avala and Zagreb. Although you will not understand, it is not the time to explain now, that time will come.

And Nostradamus said:

> —*His renown, praise, rule and power will grow, by land and by sea.*

Long ago all of this started with the woman, Razija Grgic, and today there are millions of people.

Nostradamus saw that a new birth would happen.

I can freely say that both here in Croatia, and throughout my numerous travels across Western Europe, great masses await. From one day to the next, they multiply like fish in the sea, like birds in the forest, like ants and like bees when they swarm.

People are waking up, accompanying and following me. It is enough to be near me and to be able to feel the joy, happiness, love and gladness.

Why they love me, and why you love me, you should ask yourself.

IT IS SO AND SO IT WILL BE

I worked all day yesterday, as the day before yesterday, and today. Until moments ago, I had people around me, all day, and even now the visitors listen for what I will continue to say.

Please, I would like to remind you briefly about the time when I was on that step and I came to the crown, to my spiritual father, to the Creator. And when he gave all of this to me, he told me, as I published in my books, that I have been given 23.5 million people, as well as 2,650,000,000 people. I was slandered at the time, and I would not wish this on anyone. As you can see, I overcame everything and brought everything into place.

I can freely say that the prophecies cannot be changed. A prophecy must come to pass, and so it should be. I also saw the time, the Golden time, the time that comes. I have told people, and some believe, but some still do not.

I will just briefly say, whoever believes is fortunate. They will find shelter under one of three Cross-Mountains. Those who take refuge, treasure it, and those who do not will repent. I really cannot see aid for those with this regret.

I have worked a great deal until now, informing you about the horrors and wonders of the earthly world. I said the time of earthquakes is coming, and has this indeed not happened?

The earthquakes have only just begun; I can see the earth opening up and living people falling into the ground. These are the horrors that I see.

I said there would be horrors and wonders. I have spoken about people being confined, that a brother will shoot at his brother, and a son at his father. So too, the time is coming when the negative energy will re-locate to another planet, since its days on Earth are over.

Wars always start in such places where there is something boiling under the ground. We, as people, call this hell. This is the pot where a man is thrown into boiling oil, namely the spirit of the person. In these places there is always an oil site.

I am using this introductory section to open the door a bit and tell you more closely where we all shall be passing, and what awaits us in the brighter future. The wars are, as I have already written, drastically switching to America and partially leaving Europe.

I cannot illustrate all the things I see, what it is that is coming and what awaits this agonizing humanity. All this will last until the day when humanity awakens. Awakening will not happen until the appearance of the people from Atlantis. They will come, and they even come today. I have already informed you about the places where we can see each other. They journey on the path of light. Their vessels travel at the speed of light. Please, they are a great and advanced civilization. This much I want to tell you, it is that which we shall see in this whiteness and purity.

I will tell you. You must read between the lines. I will never allow myself to impose, and lead you to places where you are unable to enter.

As you interpret me, you will be answering your own questions.

WHAT I HAVE SEEN WITH MY SPIRITUAL EYES

From time immemorial to the present day, there have always been prophets. They existed before me and now I come to tell the future and let that future be realized.

All my visions come to me of themselves; I see the future of man, an individual, of entire nations, of the entire planet. Each and every astral travel vision occurs at the time of my rest, between one and four o'clock in the afternoon, or one and four o'clock in the morning.

I SEE:
New York has been shown to me as one of the largest cities in the world, and it will be judged by fire. It will pay its dues for punishment as no other city on this planet. It will pay a punishment for that which was assigned to one of its mayors, who committed one of the greatest sins, an incestuous one.

Water will also appear, hot and dangerous, which will spring out of the ground and will, together with fire, be the judge of the city.

I SEE:
When the flames of the war calm down in the areas of former Yugoslavia, the fire will continue to spread to the West. Wars will arise, famine, and volcanoes will also awaken, for every 7,500 years Purification occurs. People will die first by weapons and then from dangerous pollution. Those that are good will be spared, their guardian angels will protect them from consuming dangerous foods and drinks, and deep wells will save the people from extinction. The Purification lasts for a few human years.

I SEE:
Germany shakes, Austria shakes, the grounds of Dalmatia also tremble, and parts of France. The entire planet is shaking and volcanoes erupt. Italy is in great smoke. Some countries are spared.

I SEE:
Arab countries unite, and the United States has great problems because of racial stirs. What is more, it will be worse in America than it was in former Yugoslavia.

I SEE:

The white, yellow and black ants are fighting. The battle is terrible. The yellow ones seem not to be from this planet, because they are so powerful. The yellow ants are quick in pushing out the white and black ones. The new civilization takes away the losses, and begins with these losses, once the killing ceases. Then peace will reign, which will last for 650 human years.

I SEE:

The grounds shake beneath Istanbul, Turkey. Something wicked is boiling, but in the shake-up something returns, which was previously taken. Great famine and major upheaval await Albania. The situation will be changeable, a little good, a little bad, but with many infirm. Greece is a land of the gods since antiquity, and God never abandons it, always preserving and keeping it in all civilizations, including the new civilization to come.

I SEE:

The German grounds shutter, there will be great changes and alterations in politics, but one city is all in flames and dust. I see Brazil at war. It is a war with the Indians, using primitive weapons—spears and arrows—they attack and come out of the green thickets of the impenetrable forests.

I SEE:

In a short span of time, Islam will strike at Christianity. I see great warlords rising, I see a black man secretly gathering Islam against Christianity, I see quarrels between people, I see the end of the church.

Now, at this time you will ask me:

—*Well, Mr. Prokić, is this not the twentieth century, when people can manage themselves, and not engage in fighting and wars?*

I would say the following: This phase must pass. What happened in former Yugoslavia was a game compared to what is coming.

I SEE:
Great accidents, the Vatican, Rome, Italy burning. America is in flames.

I SEE:
Earthquakes, volcanoes, epidemics. I see a swarm of green grasshoppers that fly—a dangerous vermin.

A long time ago I described serious illnesses. Now, I describe horrors.

I SEE:
Everywhere, the scent of flowers is disappearing, everything is becoming confined and unclear.

I see the new age coming.

I emphasize that this time will come, and it will last for 850 human years. During that time, an immortal will be born. This is a time of grace, because God wills it so. Although many have grown distant from God, during these 850 years, they will come back to him.

Blindness and hatred will disappear, and the time of pilgrimage and faith will return. I have seen one nation within today's Catholic world, which has unknowingly been enchanted. It was given Good, but it did not know how to make use of it. Once it wakes up from the dream, it will know how long it had to sleep as a punishment. It has already started to awaken. Which nation it is, the people themselves will reveal.

Also, I see another nation, which follows Mohammad, given over to loot, steal, take and commit the greatest evil since the world began, and it even builds a castle out of human skulls. This castle will have a high cost, for out of the masses of this nation, only a few of those chosen will remain in physical life. But they will bring salvation in the name of their countrymen. They will be forgiven, and those who remain will combine with others in the near future. From the capital city, hatred will disappear and it will turn into a city of love, which will emanate love throughout the entire world.

Everyone announces that the year 2000 is a milestone in the life of humankind. But this astral year began at the time of the war in Croatia, which had to occur because this was also one of God's purifications, and was meant to destroy the evil impulse which governed it before.

Except for individuals who have blood on their hands, when the war ceases, all these nations will reconcile and live in grace and love. There will be room for everyone, but not for those who love money more than they do themselves. They will have to go, because through money, the negative energy has taken over their thoughts.

All that I have brought forth here, I have watched and experienced in my astral journeys and seen with my spiritual eyes.

THE CROATIAN PROPHECY

How come I know future events? The answer was given to me in my visions: someone else is talking through my mouth. And who is this someone else? Who are they who watch over me?

No matter how much people run away from the truth, it is always right next to each of us. There is no death without the time of death arranged in advance, and it cannot be avoided. It is no consolation, but prophetic truth.

As far as it is known in Croatia, there have not been any great and notable prophets, nor notable original writings or books by them. Even the most famous prophecy of the Croats is basically doubtful. It is a prophecy that reads:

>*—Croatia will be happy and independent when a descendant of the king, who cursed Croatia and the Croats, rules it!*

The prophecy relates to King Dmitar Zvonimir, who was allegedly murdered by Croats on Blackbird's Field near Knin.

His alleged curse, which is basically this prophecy, was uttered before he died.

King Zvonimir ruled in the eleventh century, and since he had no direct male descendants, his roots to the present day are actually impossible to follow.

So, it is not difficult to conclude that the only reasonable response to this prophecy would be ... never!

However, it is not irrelevant to mention that this alleged prophecy spread throughout the Kingdom of Yugoslavia, through word of mouth, which may show that this inaccuracy only served the politics of its day, and has nothing in common with true prophecy.

I pass on my prophecies and visions faithfully. To see the destiny of others and pass it on to them is something I consider great. Although, some descriptions are incredibly clear and precisely defined, there are those that are multi-layered symbols with possible meanings, which transform into a labyrinth of wanderings, where the exit, or a concrete solution, is out of sight. Therefore, I leave my readers to attempt to interpret my visions of the future to the best of their ability.

At the same time, I also pose a challenge to those who are professionally engaged in figuring out prophecies.

Precisely because of their authenticity, my prophecies have a special value. Actually, this is the first comprehensive prophecy book in Croatia, brought forth in the classic prophetic manner.

The war on the grounds of former Yugoslavia calms down and it disappears. In Zagreb, nothing dangerous will happen again.

But, in the city under Sljeme, there is a young man in his forties. He does not wear glasses. When he comes to power, the people will love him, and he will also give much to the Croats. He is of a ruling lineage, but does not know it. His reign will be one of peace and well being, and he will be loved by God.

One town in Croatia will become known for some cure, which will appear in it. This regards a Croatian town near the sea. The whole world will hear of it, and the remedy that will come out will provide a worldwide cure. When this comes true, then immediately, in one of the nations of former Yugoslavia, a woman will rule, who will be celebrated. Just as the young man of the Croats, she will also bring peace and well being to this nation.

On the grounds of former Yugoslavia, one nation will be persecuted. They shall flee, migrate and become homeless—like the Gypsies, a wandering people without a homeland.

In one country, unseen famine will take over and many innocent victims will fall. I see the leader of that nation dead, killed by his own people in rage. When there is peace in this country, the famine will immediately disappear.

In Serbia, the rule will be taken over by someone from the Nemanjic lineage. One country full of people and nationalities will be the first to be given God's grace and everything will radically change.

A long time ago—the event took place in 1986— it was ordered that I be killed, and I have already described this in my books. At that time, I experienced clinical death and from then on I began seeing the near and distant future, and so I talked to people as much as I could.

I have already published about this crisis before it happened. I publicly stated that there would come a time when Yugoslavia would break apart.

They laughed at me.

As the first critic was my wife, she said:

> —*Ivica, don't blather on like that, be careful so you don't get*

arrested. Who could do all this?!

I told her:

> —*But Mara, bombs will fall on Zagreb. People will come who will demolish it all and there will be a great turmoil of war with hatred between the people.*
>
> *There will be an accident in the mines of Aleksinac.*
>
> *An earthquake will strike Zagreb but there will be no damage. A whirlwind of war will take many lives.*

I kept saying:

> —*A man with glasses will come to rule.*

Please, my prophecies have all come true. It all happened, just as I said. I also stated publicly in an article that the war in Croatia ends in January 1993. A long time ago, it was published in *Vikend*; that the blue helmets would come.

At the time, you read my words before the war and all this happened; these are prophecies that have come true and you know them well.

I said: Various diseases, plagues and cholera will appear. And this, too, was published.

I said: The country will be torn to pieces. There will be famine, uproars and uprisings. The time is approaching, we are watching it develop and we will experience it.

72

Please, life force is emanating from the Sun and helps us all to sustain life, humans and animals, as well as worms and ants.

The day is not far off when people will realize. Everyone will see and feel it, even those who doubted will believe and atone.

THE THREE CROSS-MOUNTAINS

At the crack of dawn, a mass of people gathered together at a place known to me. There are all kinds of people, both honest and dishonest, young and old.

A Serbian woman comes with her husband, who has green eyes. She makes love with him in front of everyone. The people are pushing and watching, but in the meantime, there are crooks and pickpockets among the crowd that take this opportunity to steal on all sides. An airplane is brought for her, and she is the pilot. She takes off together with her husband, and over our heads performs stunts, like at an air show. Then she lands. Everyone is euphoric and impressed, but nobody talks to her, except me.

I tell her:

>—*You are fortunate, you can do anything, but you cannot bear children. You will have two adopted children, but none of your own blood!*

Then, she takes off with her airplane again, showing what she knows and is capable of doing, and then flies towards Belgrade. As soon as she has flown away, a bird appears from the Sun and slowly descends lower and lower. All those present are struck mute

73

and become numb. Even the thieves stop stealing, while watching the bird that is approaching.

This bird is similar to some kind of an aircraft that does not exist in the physical human world. It makes the sound of strange cries, and amongst everyone, only I can understand them. When the bird descends low enough, I grab onto its body and it takes off, carrying me into the heights.

It tells me the following:

> —*That plane that flew until I arrived, it was the old order and the old civilization, the old construct of the world. After it, I came, the new civilization.*
>
> *You can see for yourself, as in any change, there are always those who are honest and those dishonest. They all were waiting for me, for they knew I would come. They all thought to themselves that I would take them with me, but I only took you along. I have shown that you are the chosen one, and you are marked with a cross on your forehead.*
>
> *Remember, three cities under the three mountains are marked protected, with the cross. One of them is Kruševac, the second Belgrade, and the third, Zagreb. Zagreb has been given to you along with Sljeme. Here, Heaven protects everything that lies underneath it.*
>
> *Remember, Belgrade is guarded by a male woman. A man who has been surgically transformed into a woman, a female being! That being could only rise up to the sixth door, because that was the airplane's range. You are given all thirteen doors and you may open them all. At the sixth door, the civilization, which has*

lasted until now, ends. The people I have taken you from will disappear in the same way as they came.

Remember, you have been given everything, and you know everything. Return and keep it safe, you have been entrusted!

I saw that something would happen around the city of Kruševac in Serbia, and I also see it soon becoming the capital of Serbia.

And it was revealed to me:

—The mountain you escaped from, this is Jastrebac, and it is one of the three Cross-Mountains guarded with crosses, each of which will save many living human heads. On these mountains, the flora is completely intact. As proof to my claim, any person may see this world of plants here and attest to this fact.

Each and every one taking shelter under any one of these three mountains will be spared. They will be able to observe how others starve because of the harsh climate conditions, wars, accidents and everything else that saddens a person.

Because here, on a Cross-Mountain, there can be no conflicts of war, the air cannot be polluted, and no disease or epidemics can exist. On the contrary, all that is needed to uphold life and maintain survival is situated here. This is a sacred place of special importance in this transitional time—the time of the change of civilizations. I have been told that this is where the beginning of the new civilization lies.

The first Cross-Mountain is located in Serbia.

This is Mount Jastrebac, which stretches between Kruševac and Niš. Because of the proximity to the Kruševac Cross-Mountain, it will play an important role in the near future. Mount Jastrebac has a great sign and it is closely tied to Medvednica. This is the reason for the war between Serbs and Croats, and I owe you an explanation of that war.

On this mountain, there is a church, which stores the bones of a corpse, dating back to the first year of Christianity. Those bones were not to be touched by anyone until the year 2000. At the exact moment when the bones were touched, I was shown that great detonations would occur between the inception and the third Cross-Mountain—Medvednica.

It all came true. Detonation occurred, which even last to this day and will continue until a great cross appears upon Mount Jastrebac. From that cross will arise an explanation for the civilization to come. This day is not far away. Everyone alive will be able to see that which has been awaited for 2000 years; this will be the moment that will reconcile all Christianity, and Mohammed will lose many of his followers, who were forcibly converted to Islam. They will be forgiven and they will return to Christianity once again. I must clarify that this relates to the Muslim people living in the area of former Yugoslavia.

The second Cross-Mountain is Avala, near Belgrade.

This one is also a holy mountain, and although not protected by a saint, it is still protected. It is guarded by a woman who I know little about, because I did not get a complete image in my visions.

The third Cross-Mountain is Medvednica, near Zagreb.

I have seen everything about this mountain, and I will describe the events that take place upon it. It is protected and guarded by God, Himself. Medvednica is hard to keep safe because this is where the entrance is to the underground world. In its past, Zagreb has been attacked many times, but as you can see for yourself, it has been preserved. The people are not actually aware of what goes on here, for what is happening is not accessible to their eyes. In order to make all of this clearer, I will give you the simplest example, so that it is understandable for everyone.

It is known that during autumn and winter days, Zagreb is often covered in fog. Did anyone ever ask why this fog takes place here? It is believed that strong evaporation happens because of the lowlands. This is not correct, and it is not the only reason. I have been given an explanation of why the most fog takes place around Zagreb; the fog prevents people from seeing the work that is being done by the underground world. Because of the great power of the Sun, the underground world cannot act in spring and summer, since the Sun's rays destroy its influence. This is why it operates in autumn and winter, but the fog protects the people.

Every 7,500 years, purification occurs on the Earth, and we are now entering this period of time. The purification started in May 1992 in the following ways: drought, heat and earthquakes . . . eventually, water will run out, general pollution will occur, yet, all who harbor under any one of the three Cross-Mountains will be safe. This applies to all humankind, and not just a specific country.

So, the negative energy is going to depart!

For now it has found a habitat on American soil, where it will fully carry out its goal. The aim is to alienate Christianity and Islam. Therefore, on the grounds of America, hellfire and war will come.

Once its goal has been accomplished, the negative energy will go to a different planet, where it will remain. Then, tranquility will reign over the Earth. Nature will come alive and everything will be equally protected, just as the three Cross-Mountains are. Prosperity and peace will come for all mankind.

With this, I would like to conclude this chapter on the three mountains of the Cross, and I, as the God-given chosen one for Medvednica, advise all people not to wish harm to anyone. What you wish for yourself, let everyone also wish for each other, and then there will be no more conflicts amongst people.

A TSARIAN CURSE

I note again that Kruševac will be the capital of Serbia. It plays a part historically in all of this with much contributed by Tsar Lazar.

I see a great curse on the Serbian nation, which was made by a little girl, during the reign of Tsar Lazar. Ever since then until the present time, the Serbs could do nothing else but constantly go to war. They have become the most war-like nation in the world. This curse should now be forgiven, and right at the time of the change of civilizations. I see the little girl; she has already been born to a Serbian father and Croatian mother. She will reconcile these two nations by saying only two words.

The curse shall be removed from this nation, and it will be blood-bound with the Croatian people. Croats and Serbs will make peace and they will never fall out again. Great love will rule over these two nations in the Balkans.

CLOSE ENCOUNTERS

Very soon, representatives from other civilizations will arrive from other planets in the universe, and come into contact with us, mortal physical people. The aliens come from three planets, which are ruled by different gods, because every planet has its own god ruling over it. Likewise, God is not something distant from us, he is always close at hand, and we are all walking in his kingdom without actually knowing it.

People from other planets, therefore, are coming.

They are not people of flesh and blood; they are programmed, but intelligent creatures. They are representatives of advanced and developed cultures and civilizations, and two types come first. One of them leaps like a grasshopper. They come to us in strange devices, like bright spheres and they are faster than light.

In a short span of human time an encounter with these aliens will take place. Their arrival will encourage us, the people from Earth, to start travelling through the universe and to go to other planets. We will quickly find a common language with these visitors enabling us to understand and communicate with each other.

As I said, two kinds arrive. The first leap, while the second do not walk, but hover above the ground. Representatives from a third planet will also come a little later.

Representatives from one of those advanced civilizations will leave us, just as fast as they arrived. They are, however, constantly visiting, examining and studying us.

They used to live on our Earth, and their civilization evolved in the continental areas that are now under the ice. As a punishment, they were taken away from the Earth, and delivered into the hands of the positive energy that rules over their once new, and now old homeland. They return to find what their ancestors left behind under the ice.

What has been left behind, physical people cannot find with their present capabilities and devices. Ice does not harm these visitors at all. They have been visiting us every once in a while for thousands of years, looking for something that is still undiscovered knowledge to us. They are the descendants of the civilization that ruled over the Earth before this one, our current civilization.

And, the realm of those who live on the third planet, whose representatives will come after those who leap and those who hover, also used to inhabit the Earth. It disappeared in a great flood and was completely destroyed. This civilization once flourished on the continent that existed in the past, a continent which no longer exists. It is hiding under the thick layers of the ocean waters. The people of this missing continent relocated to another planet so they were partially saved. There are several timeless routes leading from our Earth, bridging our planet to their planet.

One of the entrances is an area called the Devil's triangle. This is an area of special magnetic time. Whoever enters this area is transported in the same instant with unprecedented speed to that other planet. Clairvoyant individuals can confirm that this is indeed the case.

This planet, where descendants of the inhabitants of the destroyed earth civilization reside, along with those who have been caught in the net of magnetic time, is one of the three planets from which the visitors come or will start coming.

Whether all of the residents from that planet return to Mother Earth one day; this remains to be seen.

People have divided and separated from one another. Those who have chosen to serve money, the Golden calf, have lost themselves, because money does not make one happy. Love is a gift that cannot be bought with money.

I see three healing sources in the area of former Yugoslavia. I know where they are, but I do not wish to give them away since they are to be discovered by others. Although presently unknown, these three healing sources have been assigned to all mankind and they will heal a number of diseases, including infertility.

Earthquakes will shake the earth until the time when a clear sign for everyone to see appears in the sky. Once the sign shines forth, there will never be any more earthquakes.

THE CRYSTAL CITY

Faith in God will continue to grow stronger, and that time is at your doorstep. In Europe, there will be a pilgrimage site, which will be especially celebrated, for believers will flock there in masses. It will be a place of special brightness.

Very soon, a city will be built, which at the present does not have a foundation. But in the heavens, it is already being built. There will be a great many inhabitants here, many vehicles, gardens and palaces. There will be transport vehicles on its streets, similar to trams, although these are not trams. This city will be made of transparent crystal. It will stretch across the hills, and over time, many cures will be discovered for incurable diseases of our day.

A church will be built in this city, where the flame of the new civilization will blaze. People from all over the world will make pilgrimages here. In this crystal city, all kinds of wonders will take place every day. From it, something will spring that cannot be seen anywhere else, and here the doors of Heaven will open. And it is from this new city, that one will be able to look at civilizations on other planets throughout the universe. All that is found on the earth, and everything that exists on it, will be encountered in this city. For, this city will live eternally, and it will be the city of love and truth.

It was not given for me to know its name, but I was shown this city; it is a crystal city, the likeness of which has never been seen before anywhere in this civilization.

I know the place where it will be, but it cannot be disclosed so soon. Please note that it is already being built in the heavens, and soon its replica shall shine forth in our physical world on earth.

COUNTRIES IN THE SKY

In the sky, countries look like beehives 100 meters in length and 50 meters in width. I have seen them all on my astral journeys. They are built as a home to a country.

People do not live in these buildings in the sky, bees do. Each dwelling, which represents a country in the physical world, receives one capital in which there is a cross and a candle, and only then a flag. In every dwelling, aside from one queen bee, there are several subordinate ones. These correspond to the rulers and statesmen on earth.

At every entrance to such a dwelling, garrisons of guards protect and safeguard the entrance from intruders. Every dwelling—country—is given everything it needs for survival and long life.

As it is on earth, so it is there, in the heavens, in these domiciles. All that would happen on earth happens beforehand in these dwellings—these countries represented in the sky.

Just as on earth, Evil can also disrupt the harmony in these dwellings in the sky. Then civil wars break out, and when hatred is sown between two swarms of bees, then war and bloodshed will erupt between the countries.

What did I see in the sky in the dwelling, which used to be Yugoslavia?

I saw a swarm representing Slovenia flying out of the common dwelling. The queen bee grabbed onto a mulberry tree. The diligent working bees immediately started building a honeycomb around her. It is not complete yet, which means that Slovenia as a country is still unprotected. The mulberry tree is the base, but the honeycomb has still not formed into a dwelling, which would represent a country.

From the former common dwelling—country, the Croatian swarm of bees flew out. It has still not grabbed onto any tree, even though it is outside the common dwelling. It is not yet building itself a honeycomb, the queen bee has still not decided where to land, or what to grab onto.

In the dwelling, representing the remainder of former Yugoslavia, an intruder is sought after, who entered and tore everything apart. However, they are also looking for a new queen bee, because the old one can no longer lead the hive. The roof of the house has been removed, and the bees are fighting and killing each other.

The war between bees—which parallels that which is taking place among the people on earth—can be stopped when the prior punishments are completed. Namely, when the people of one county sincerely repent, then their dwelling will receive a roof and will become protected.

Disease, war and all the tribulations that occur in a dwelling cannot be passed on to others. They can only be passed on by negative energy, and only in the form of a punishment for committed sins. As soon as a dwelling becomes roofless, it also becomes unprotected. Then epidemics, war, disease and all other adversities occur.

Every country is also given the mentality of its residents. If one beehive is overcome with an excessive proneness to temptation and material rewards, it becomes cursed.

This is simultaneously reflected in the events unfolding in our physical life on earth.

Furthermore, soon in these areas, after all of this is over the prophecies hold that joy, goodwill and happiness will reign. Those who get to see this time shall be very fortunate and I wish them much luck.

CHAPTER 4

THE TRUTH ABOUT
THE VISIONS

THERE ARE NO COINCIDENCES

On my astral journeys, I have seen everything that has been granted for me to see. I have seen the life of every human being, and that life only comes down to a flame.

Upon this earthly world, there are no coincidences.

I have brought back many things from these journeys and I will speak amply about them. A person has no secrets. If you are wondering how come an individual cannot have his own secrets, it is because the earth vowed to the Heavens that all the secrets would be known.

This is true in the following way. When a man goes to do something that he does not want others to know about, he thinks that he can get away with it, because no one will see him. But, this is really trying to cheat because, as I said, our Spirit guide is standing to our right, and negative energy comes to us from the left side.

I have already written that every building, every village and every city has guards. They are constantly observing and watching all that goes on, including when the negative energy, through an evil minion, successfully lulls a Spirit guide to sleep by bewitching him or her. At that time, a man is willing to do anything, thinking there are no witnesses, and this leads him to commit evil. When a man is subject to this influence he makes mistakes. Divine guardians see all of this and the man is exposed.

There simply can be no secrets.

Likewise, when a man is very good, when he thinks good thoughts and does good works, this is also noted and recorded, and this seal can never be erased and that goodness always comes back to him. There is no punishment for good individuals; they belong to God and Truth. On astral journeys, many things may be seen, but they are especially shown to individuals who return with knowledge that others cannot know. Yet, though these individuals see, it is not spoken to them. Such people are traveling, they have been given the ability to do so, and it is normal to be tempted by it.

Here, I would note one of my astral journeys where I saw someone's entire secret of what was going to come, arriving in a very short span of time. It is in progress and it belongs to the new civilization, which is just about to knock on our door. On this trip, I saw people from different planets meeting, and the earth giving birth, with a complete fertilization given to her by the light of the Sun. Every planet has its own mother and father. So, this is our mother Earth, and our father Sun.

Everything is strictly predetermined and everyone lives according to their destiny; a human being, village, city, country, as well as the entire planet.

I repeat again, there are no coincidences.

SO IT BEGAN

When I think back now, my beginning was associated with dreams.

I would lie down, rest, fall asleep and dream, with the dreams in color. At first, I was convinced they were all only dreams, and that all people dream just as I do. But soon I realized that it was not merely dreaming, but rather my inner, contemplative, astral body separating from my physical one. And, then I go into the future, to events that are yet to come, which sometimes are shown to me openly, but sometimes in symbols and specific signs.

I found out that these were future events immediately after, my so-called dreams, started to come true. Then, I discovered that they were not dreams. These were visions. The moment that I realized that I was having visions, and that I received them on these astral journeys of the soul, they became more frequent. When these journeys covered the more distant future, then the symbols of upcoming events became more intricate with content.

In the beginning, everything I saw in these visions during astral travel related to events that would happen to me. Some messages were very simple. For example, in one of them I saw myself on a bicycle coming into the village to buy land. I began to ask if anyone around was selling land. I knew the names of people I had never seen before, and they took me to a woman. I then paid her six million dinars, the currency at the time, leaving me to owe her nine more.

As soon as the vision ended, I woke my wife up, though it was the middle of the night, and told her everything. When dawn came a bodiless hand appeared, which was inviting me somewhere. I sat on my bike and started following it. It led me to Žitnjak, directly to the woman I had seen in my vision, and for precisely that same amount of money, I bought a piece of land that I still have today.

Over time, the meanings of the visions started to change. The foretelling of what would happen to me transfigured into prophecies regarding the future of Croatia and beyond.

Visions in astral travel consciousness, without the physical body, also pointed to some truths about the general, invisible world of human destiny.

Gradually, I was able to know more than others knew. I especially remember the vision I saw on October 20, 1982. I was told that I had to make the final payment on the land where I was living and build a house on it.

When I did this, something inexplicable happened; my newly built house turned into a fish, which then transformed into a girl dressed in oriental garb.

She looked at me and said:

> —*Kill me! Then you will become the ruler of this earth. Only you can kill me and no one else!*

In detail, she explained the way in which I had to kill her. Following her instructions, I hit her with a stone on her left thigh, and then on her head, but she still continued to live.

Then she advised:

—*Tear out my heart!*

And, I really did tear out her heart. Finally, she was dead. All of a sudden, I found myself surrounded by police. Although I was apprehended for committing the crime, I surrendered to fate. I was aware that by killing this girl, I was actually killing Evil.

It was one of my first visions and it kept re-occurring for eight years. Its symbols were not revealed until it became a reality.

So it began.

MY FIRST VISION

My first vision occurred on July 14, 1963, when I was 13 years old. All of my family went to the market, and I was left behind at home as a punishment. I reached for the poison, wanting to kill myself, and then a woman dressed in black stood in front of me and said:

—*Do not do it. You will live in a place where people are as numerous as ants.*

In the vision, I am in Zagreb and I am walking in a meadow. I then find a goose egg and hear an inner voice telling me to take it with me. I take it and give it to my wife, and immediately a light carries me to another location. It is a place similar to a prison and I must remain there for 28 astral hours, that is, 28 physical, human days.

89

A guard comes by asking about my last name. I notice that I have another 14 astral hours left to be released, but he immediately writes me a note for discharge. A last name is written down, but that name remains a secret.

As soon as I am out, I hear the cries of a little girl being held captive high in the mountains. She cries out seeking my help and I hear her say that although I am not her physical father, and my wife is not her physical mother, I have to save and adopt her.

I do not hesitate and immediately run to free her. She is being kept by a man in sheepskin and two women who guard and torture her. Coming up to a log cabin, I find the little girl in it, lying on the floorboards. I go to get her, and she has a lump on her face. At this point, we are next to my wife and a neighbor, and they take the young girl.

I leave.

I pass a house, whose residents present me with walnuts, plumbs and other confections, because I have saved the child who was different from all of the other children.

CONSCIOUNESS WITHOUT A BODY

At least ten times, I have had the opportunity to see a duplicate of myself, simultaneously in several places. I was even seen by others in one place, while I was simultaneously seen in front of witnesses at a completely different location, miles away.

When I return from my astral journeys and am pulled back into my physical body, that merging is always very sweet for me. It has a delight that will remain in my body even when I open my eyes, and start living in my physically present life. That moment of connection is always the sweetest part of these experiences.

Throughout my numerous journeys of astral consciousness without my body, there have been various visions, and some of them have impressed me greatly.

In one of the visions, a young man came to me to be healed. He had problems with potency. When I began healing him with bioenergy, he closed his eyes. When I laid my palms on his eyelids, he told me about an image of a great crown appearing to him.

I continued holding my palms on his eyes, and decided to see whether he could also see those same visions that I had seen. He started to speak about everything that moved in front of his eyes.

And, these were my visions!

There is no way he could have found out about them earlier, because I literally had not told anyone about them at the time.

When I returned home, I sat my young daughter down and put my palms on her closed eyes, asking her what she could see. She started telling me about things that surprised me. Over the next few days, I laid palms on the closed eyes of everyone who came seeking my healing help.

They all talked about visions that only I had seen and no one else! As a rule, everything that was described was exactly word for word, event for event, image for image!

Then, a woman came to me, and in the same way, I tried to usher her into the world of my visions, which only I formerly saw. But, despite all my best efforts, she could see nothing.

I wondered about this fact, until it was explained to me in a vision on one of the astral journeys; she had a connection with the underworld kingdom. Such people are unable to see what others are trying to give to them, and since this vision, I do not help these people.

There were more unusual events at that time. For example, a woman from Sisak came to me and said:

—Mr. Ivica, you were in my house last night!

I replied:

—Oh no, it can't be. I don't even know where you live!

But to convince me further, she persisted:

—I'm telling you, it's true! I was lying down and you approached me and said that I, Milka, was now completely healthy and would have no more pain. You warned me that in a year's time, here in Sisak, houses would burn down and I would have to flee.

I remembered this conversation only when the conflicts in Croatia began, even though the conversation happened in August of 1990. In this unusual way, that direct message about future events sadly came true.

SPIRIT GUIDE

A Spirit guide is not only given to each human being in this physical world, but also to each nation. Such a Spirit guide protects the entire area of a country with its energy.

Croatia has its own special Spirit guide, and the one that used to hover above former Yugoslavia has disappeared. A country's Spirit guide has an impact on all the residents in the area under its care. The Spirit guide of a nation or a country is stronger than any individual's Spirit guide.

Spirit guides of nations or countries may be charged with either positive or negative energy, depending on whether the people in that country are cursed with a punishment or not. When the entire nation is sentenced to a punishment, then the Spirit guide is vicious and short-tempered and the country under his rule immediately breaks out in war, bloodshed and all kinds of conflicts. The rule of this evil Spirit guide is not for an endless length. Measured in human physical time, the rule lasts between two and a half to five years. Once its time of rule runs out, the negative Spirit guide leaves and positive energy takes its place, calming everything down and stopping the adversities.

What is a Spirit guide to me?

It is, as I stated before, Strength. It can be found in each and every one of us, but also above us. It cannot be seen with our physical eyes, but it leads our physical body. It takes the form of light and one cannot live without it.

When an individual suddenly falls ill, it is a sign that his Spirit guide has become intoxicated and fallen asleep. As soon as the

Spirit guide ceases to function, the robot—our physical, human body—also ceases to function. The Spirit guide is actually the human soul.

I was given to see myself arriving to an unknown city where I had to listen to lectures for two astral hours, and learn like a student. In the crowds of people, it was not hard for me to detect the spies of the underworld kingdom, who were sent to kill me. I recognized them because they do not have blood inside of them. They would have managed to kill me, were it not for the protection of three young Gypsies. They told me:

—*Master, we have to protect you!*

They led me, and even though they were only children, they knew more than I did. This did not surprise me at all, although in physical life it would be very unusual. On the way, I came to know that the Gypsy people are a nation cursed by God. They have been given to know many things, but because of this Divine curse, they are scattered throughout the world, so that we may learn and get to know ourselves through their homeless situation. I knew that their Divine curse was ending, and they would have their own country, because a dwelling in the sky was already being built for them.

As we kept on going further and further, the underworld conspirators and spies followed and harassed us. When we reached the end of our road, a river spilled in front of us with a tall mountain looming. The Gypsy children directed me to cross the river and go to the top of the mountain, while they kept my pursuers from following me. I crossed the river without difficulty, and then began the strenuous climb. The rock faces of the mountain were slippery, without roads or paths, so I climbed the trackless terrain, sliding and falling, then rising up again to continue forward.

Once I had ascended halfway up the mountain, I turned around to look back. The three Gypsy children had transformed, taking on my characteristics, and were swimming in the river luring the pursuers to catch them. The pursuers really did jump into the water trying to catch them, but in doing so they all drowned, because the water was deadly to them. I knew there would be no more tormenters.

I continued climbing to the top of the mountain in a much more peaceful way. And once I finally reached the summit, there was a small, charming church, about sixteen square meters in size, with four doors appearing in archways, rather than doorways. I approached the church from the west.

My Spirit guide then told me:

>—*Enter, inside there is a corpse in a coffin that lies here dead for 2000 years.*

I looked around, and on the north wall there was a painting of a 36-year-old woman, who I did not know.

Then, my Spirit guide continued:

>—*Put your right hand on the coffin!*

I obeyed and when the wood of the coffin creaked, I flinched and shivered in discomfort. The lid began to open. I was afraid I would suffocate from the stench with the lid rising. But it did not smell at all. I saw the skeleton, which had a large amount of gold coins around the neck.

I was told:

> —*Do not take anything from the grave because there is only dust inside of it!*

There was rumbling all around me, and the air began to boil. Then, the Voice continued:

> —*You did what you had to do, now run, because all of this will disappear!*

I ran toward the east side, I ran and ran, and then came running up to an unknown village. I met a graying 45-year-old man, with bracelets made of maize around his wrists. He said to me:

> —*You have arrived. We have been waiting for you.*

In wonder, I asked him:

> —*How could you be waiting for me, when I have never seen you before?*

To this he answered:

> —*You see; your journey to S. is 100 thousand dinars and 4 million to Zagreb.*

> —*I don't have any money. I can only pay you back later, in Zagreb.*

The overall purpose of the Spirit guide's actions is for people to see with their heart and feelings, and not only with their physical, materialistic senses.

JUMP INTO THE DISTANCE

On my frequent astral journeys, I see visions of future events. The visions begin as soon as I see the opening of the doors, which do not exist in the physical world.

This means that those doors cannot be seen by anyone else but me. At the moment when the doors open for me, I leave my physical body, and set out to begin an astral travel.

At one time this only happened in my dreams, while I rested. Now, it happens while I am on the go, when I am walking down the street. All of a sudden, I see a bright light and it carries me to the event that I need to see.

I must emphasize here that my visions are related to events in the future.

If I look through an open door, then it is about an event in the near future. However, if I look through a window, the event relates to the distant future.

VISION:

I lay down around midnight and immediately started to astral travel, finding myself in a carriage with a child. My arms are full of packages and as we pass by a river, four chickens fall out of my arms into the river. On this journey, I am followed by a bitch that jumped into the river and dragged them out, but beside her was a fish that also helped with the rescue. Then, the river dried up before my eyes, and at the bottom lay a fish as big as a house. It spoke in a human voice, turning into a Turkish bull, with a series of gold coins around its neck:

> —*If you kill me you will rule the world! If you do not kill me, you will not!*

And the vision ceased.

VISION:

In the night of September 2 to 3, 1990, I lay back in my bed and my soul began astral travelling. I saw a pregnant woman with a black child in her stomach. He wanted to be born through the navel. I caressed the stomach and the child was born in the normal manner.

I did not know what this vision could mean, so I asked my Spirit guide to clarify it for me. I was told there would be an earthquake in Zagreb at 12:55 p.m. I was also told that this was the work of negative energy. If Zagreb did not have Sljeme's protection, which is a Cross-Mountain, the houses would have collapsed, as an underground volcano would have erupted and everything would have turned into a catastrophe.

I told people who came to me for predicting the future about this vision. At least fifteen people have heard this announcement of mine, a doctor among them.

I need not say that the vision came true.

VISION:

Some visions I remember especially clearly, and among them is an astral journey from March 1990.

In the vision, it was snowing. I was in my house. I was looking at the dog. My wife was next to me, busily doing something. Suddenly, I was carried to Zagreb, to my present house. There was a big pot with laundry on the stove, and water was being heated for bathing because the water heater had broken. On one table there was a large veal shank. There were two more tables on the sides, with empty space in between them, so that one could form a horseshoe with all three tables. Suddenly, a woman arrived with her husband, and both of them were orthodox Christians.

They said:

—*We have come, baptize us. Rechristen us.*

In wonder I replied:

—*Folks, I cannot do this!*

They were surprised and asked:

—*Why not? You have been to the Heavens! You have been seen by all the people!*

With this utterance, a mass of people began to come in through the door, both known and unknown, of all religions and probable confessions.

I told them:

—*Wait a little while, your table will be set up immediately!*

I watched as Croats sat at one table, and Serbs at another, and at the third table sat Muslims. All of them talked about coming for their baptism. I told them that I would first take a bath, and then a coat was passed to me from the crowds, which I donned. I cut the meat and passed it to all the people to eat.

VISION:

I was between two raw mountains in an unknown place. The mountains stood tightly together and formed a canyon with high cliffs. After much effort, I arrived at this place. As I sat down, all of a sudden, sheep started appearing around me. There were more and more. There was a damn in the canyon, which prevented the mighty waters from flowing. Suddenly, the damn started to leak, and the rocks began cracking and it was bursting all over, and then a fierce current rushed through, destroying everything in its way and all in its path. In this current, many sheep drowned.

VISION:

This is one of my earlier visions, which has still not come true in reality, but it will:

I saw three churches, and all three were built next to each other. I watched the inner walls cracking and collapsing. The priests of all three religions were praying to God.

I heard a voice:

—You see, there is only one religion! You see, there is only one God!

Then all three churches became one. As I went out, there was a donkey with a saddle pack in front of the doors. I sat on it and behind me there was one Bosnian. We flew high into the Croatian sky and arrived above Sljeme. We passed it and went on, flying over Zagreb.

I tore a newspaper into bits and pieces and threw them over the city, explaining to the man that here, in Zagreb, I had many friends and good people, and so I threw these bits of paper for their happiness and their prosperity.

VISION:

On the night of September 19, 1990, I had an unusual vision.

Just as I lay down, a bright light appeared that fully illuminated the bedroom. This light took me out of my physical body. I was watching myself sleep. Simultaneously, I was on the bed and above it, above myself.

After I had spiritually observed my physical body in this worldly dream, that brilliant light took me through time and space. I found myself on an island and saw a guardsman on duty.

The light raised me higher, all the way to the entrance in the sky.

On the island, I was sentenced to 14 astral months in prison, and the astral journey ended on this island at the time when I was pardoned and released.

Right next to me was a huge, impregnable tower with walls so smooth that no one could climb them. Also, the tower was built in a way that not as much as a fly could exit without permission.

Even my own Spirit guide, guiding and carrying me on all my astral journeys and visions, could not get into this tower.

I realized that there was an immense secret within it, but I did not know what it was.

I was told:

>—*You will not know what you did in the tower, but there will come a time when you will consciously recall it.*

I was standing in the bushes near the road that led from this tower, and suddenly I saw 12 men with black hair exiting, and I was among them. We left and were ordered into four rows. I was the shortest amongst them all, in the second row, and counting from the beginning, in the sixth position.

A man was walking in front of us, the thirteenth one.

When we marched off, he ordered us to strip off our clothes from the upper part of our bodies to work.

He explained.

>—*Only a little bit of gymnastics and you are free!*

From all twelve of us, no one carried anything, except me. I, as the shortest one, had a small bundle with some handcrafted objects in it.

The thirteenth continued to explain:

—Now you are free and you have to go back to your registration offices! Go get your certificates!

We all went. A fat woman gave each of us certificates; they were all the same without any names. She warned us that we could live with these certificates, but we had to register at our registration offices.

Then, I was moved into an astral house. It seemed as if I had forgotten how to walk. As I made several clumsy steps, my shoe fell off. At that moment, I saw a woman.

I sharply said right to her face:

—You are the one who was destroying me, but you cannot harm me any longer!

As soon as I uttered those words, I found myself in Zagreb. The woman I spoke to was one of my neighbors. The dog was tied to a chain and barking. At that moment, a rat ran across the street, a big rat. I took something from my small bundle and threw it at the rat, killing it. Then, I was returned to the place where I had lost my shoe.

For me, this was one of the turning points in my life, even though all the symbols and meaning have not yet been revealed.

Suddenly, I was part of a crowd.

—We have been waiting for you, we have welcomed you, but now you must again set out on a journey.

Thus, I went to Zagreb, where I am now.

VISION:

I was allowed to see this. Dancing people appeared on the top of a hill and all around were houses made of glass. I was among twelve unfamiliar prisoners, eleven of us were men and there was one woman. We were all lying in a cell in one of these houses, completely isolated from the rest of the world. The glass separated us from everything else.

There was only one iron bed in the cell with a man in uniform lying on it, giving each one of us notice of when we would be released to freedom. In passing, he mentioned that the trial was to be held on the tenth day.

But all of a sudden, one of us spoke up, saying there would be no trial.

Then the cell of glass and the glass prison opened all by itself, and we were permitted to leave. A crowd of people applauded us. Everyone rejoiced.

I turned and looked, and saw an army on one side and police on the other. The military wore blue helmets that were unfamiliar to me; these were foreign people from other countries. They opened a way for us to go forward!

VISION:

I was strolling with a friend on Zrinjevac Street. Suddenly, spies from the underworld kingdom ambushed us. They locked us in a dungeon. They tortured and beat us, breaking our bones. Completely beaten up, they threw me into a cell. I was covered with bruises lying on a pallet, while in front of me stood a giant who poked at me.

He mocked:

—Where is this God of yours now to help you?!

I was tortured over and over again and endured all of it. I could not see the person in charge among these moles, since his face was constantly shadowed. At one point, the sun's rays suddenly burst through the barred window and shed light on him. I recognized his face, it belonged to the ruler of the underground world. As the sun went on shining stronger and stronger, one piece broke off from the sun, stabbed him in the back and he fell dead to the floor. The positive energy wins again. I exited the prison, and saw that many people were left jobless.

And I wondered:

—Are there really so many people secretly working for the ruler of the underworld?

VISION:

This is a vision from early in the spring of 1987.

I am sitting with four other men and we successfully negotiate the sale of my house, which actually exists in physical life. The arrangements are successful, and so I sell the house and leave satisfied.

I come out to the courtyard, which is filled with young people. Some young men are playing guitars and singing. The song gets louder and less harmonious, turning into shouting. The clamor keeps getting louder. I am afraid of it disturbing my neighbors. I ask the gathered people to disperse peacefully and they object, replying that they will only leave if I leave with them.

In a certain way, I am scared of them, so I cannot chase them away forcibly. I ask and plead with them, and I finally manage to get them to leave, but they take me along. We are all going up a hill, with me in the front. As we are climbing, I can see more clearly, and I see women and children among them. There is a constant sense of uneasiness within me, and in a suitable moment, I manage to break away and flee from them.

My wife and children, who were with us, stay as hostages. In fear, I run across a field and through the water of a river. I see a house with the outside lights on, and run to it. There I meet a neighbor, who is the landlady of that house. I tell her the troubled situation I am in and ask for help, pleading for her to hide me. I thought I was safe there, but in a short time, three men in uniform come by and I fail to recognize them. They catch me and take me up the hill.

I wonder:

—*So, even you work for them?*

I get a stingy response:

—*Yes.*

The unknown men in uniform take me to the top of the hill, and throw me onto the rocks. They torture me with a hook. Then, all of a sudden, something changes, something happens, although I cannot discern exactly what it is. But, I am aware that I have won. I have prevailed, and I am finally by myself, undisturbed and safe.

VISION:

In February 1987, I had a vision in which I was seeking an affordable family home to buy. As I was looking, I finally came across an owner selling a house at a price that suited me. There were some quiet people in the house. None of them spoke, they only observed everything. They did not get involved in the sale. The owner took me to view the grounds. At the bottom of a meadow, there was a well. Here, I noticed a swarm of bees, moving and swarming from one beehive into another. I marveled at how the bees were swarming in February.

The owner sold me the house, and as to my questions about the swarming bees, I did not get any specific answers.

VISION:

In early January 1990, I had the following vision.

I went out of the house during the day. I saw my Muslim neighbor digging a canal from his yard to the street.

—What are you digging?

Instead of answering, he said:

—Ah, I have been waiting for you!

The way he looked at me, I thought he wanted to kill me. Then, finally he explained:

—You see, last night, as I lay in bed, a light came into my house, telling me that I am not the child of my parents. I was told to take a pick and a shovel, and to dig a trench across the road until I came to a tree without branches. Here, I would dig up a metal that is worthless today, but in time will acquire tremendous value.

I was told not to keep it, but to give it to the families that will need it. Then, I would find out the true lineage of my father and mother, and I would finally become what I am, though I am not even aware of it, and what I am destined for.

—And where is the tree? I marveled.

—I don't know. Over there, the neighbor has a chestnut tree without any branches, so I will dig until I come to it and then see if I find anything or not.

After that, he went on:

>—*If I do not find the metal there, I'll dig the trench further, towards the other branchless trees.*

I told him:

>—*You're an idiot. By the time you find the branchless tree, it will be spring and the branches will all be growing. So you will not find it quickly. In the meantime, many people will get hurt.*

At this point, the vision ceased. Some days later, still in January 1990, while I was awake, a priest came to my house. After he came, and left, I lay down and took a nap.

VISION:

Suddenly, as is usually the case, I had a vision: I saw the house of my birth. Someone was warning me that I should not fall asleep because the spies of the underworld were coming. The lights immediately turned off, and people were on the watch and awake. That same priest, who was in my house in reality, walked by the windows. He came in, carrying a great needle, wanting to stab me with it. Then, I was told:

>—*Take two bottles, a green and a brown one, and when he is in front of you, smash them on the ground at his feet.*

I was waiting for the moment when I would break them. Just as I was about to shatter them, at that very moment, the priest groaned and thus prevented the breaking of the bottles.

He said:

—You see how small and weak you are!

I looked closer and noticed that on one of his legs, he had a hoof instead of a foot. I became very scared. I looked around and saw two strangers. I saw them approaching and wanting to catch me. I asked a shepherd for help, but this was futile. One of the two approached. He caught me and tried to kill me. I am aware that I am stronger than he is, and that he really desires evil because of human jealousy. I could not defend myself and so I ran.

I ran until I came to a high wall. I would have jumped over it, but it was too high. Then I remembered and called out:

—Strength, help me!

Immediately, something raised me into the air and I was carried over the wall onto the other side, to safety. I left that place and met a baker on the way, who had freshly baked bread. I wanted a bun with cheese, but he would not give it to me. I would have gone hungry were it not for a strange woman coming along who said to him:

—Let it go, give it to him. He is the man who sees.

I went on further and came by a place where I was supposed to cut down a tree. Once I had cut it down, three children arrived. Among them was my son, Alen. They lifted me and carried me into the heights. I saw many people killed and thrown into the water.

—These people opposed someone and then they were killed by

directive. By the way, their wealth was also taken away.

I was given this answer to my silent question. Then one of the boys almost fell from the heights and I cried out:

—Strength, help!

The boy managed to catch onto me, and so we went on flying further and further. I heard a voice, and it explained to me:

—You have been given to help the young and the old, so be good. You have seen where the traps are set, but do not be afraid, the houses are safe.

—That is impossible! I cried.

—No, you will see, it will be so. Stay calm.

VISION:

I came to a village and saw the place where I had previously been held captive. While I waited for the bus in order to travel on further, I saw people all around me who I know have lived in the 12th century! The bus arrives, I board and we are off.

Suddenly, I heard a voice saying to me:

—Tell your friend that you always come by means of the back way, like a thief at midnight, and never on the main road!

The vision cuts off. What was meant here, I do not know.

VISION:

In April 1990, I had a vision of a wedding in the house where I was born. My mother was passing me a white shirt, blue trousers and shoes that no one in the world possesses. She told me:

> —*These shoes are only meant for you, but this is not all. The other pair of shoes, made of crocodile skin, are already being made for you. They are not finished yet, but when they are, they will be presented to you.*

VISION:

In June 1991, I had a vision of walking from Retkovac Street towards the rail line for Zagreb-Belgrade. In passing, I came across a house in which there were three young men, crooks. They wanted to steal my shoes and with this intention, they succeeded. However, one of them was obliging towards me. He helped me and we killed the other two together. I looked in front of the house and there was a small table, where vegetables were on sale to the passers by, and among them were my shoes! They were meaning to sell them! At this point, two policemen came by and took my helper away, but not for helping me; it was for the crimes that he had previously committed.

I swore to him:

> —*I'll help you from the outside and get you out of prison!*

I was left alone. The spies of the underground world always try to inflict some kind of harm on people.

I see my son Alen in the vision, saying to me:

> —Dad, a stranger came by while you were at work. He brought a small package he found under his pillow that was meant for you. He doesn't know what it was doing under his pillow. He just said that only you could see what is inside.

But since my son was curious, he opened the package. Inside, there were seashells. As soon as they were unwrapped, they began to open, and a spirit started to come out. My son screamed and I immediately came in and destroyed the evil spirit. I knew at once that the stranger was the man who was killed earlier, which means he was a spirit from the underworld.

I explained to the child:

> —Never, my son, accept gifts from unknown strangers.

VISION:

There is another vision related to my son.

Namely, in a vision, I see him in an enclosed part of the forest behind the house. He notices that a woman is setting a man loose, who turns into a snake. Alen and his peer manage to kill the snake, but that woman turns into a snake emperor and pursues them, wanting revenge. Alen runs and calls for me. The woman now pursues my entire family, and then a great, blinding light shines out.

I am here, turning that woman into a frog, locking her in a sphere and throwing it away. Then, the evil withdraws.

VISION:

On my astral journey, I saw the "Hotel I" and I was in it, healing people. Meanwhile, under the entrance bars, a snake with two heads appears, with each of the heads hissing in different directions.

I work in front of the hotel, approach the snake and cut off both heads. They turn into harmless little snakes, and I also kill them.

I resume working, but there are prophets, healers and seers arriving in the hotel lobby. I am in charge of letting these people know who is good, and who is a fraud. Among them I notice the son of a prophetess from Sarajevo.

I turn to him:

> —*Tell your mother I admitted you, and that she must send me every third person that comes to her and she must tell everyone that I exist.*

In this vision, I see myself arriving to a former Zagreb military hospital in Dubrava. I am aware that I work here as a healer. The door is locked, and as I look for documents, I see acquaintances from the police. I give them the first piece of paper I find in my pocket, which states that I heal people. Once my working hours are completed, I notice that the piece of paper has not been returned to me. A thief is sought after in the hospital, but I must go. It's late and I turn to an acquaintance:

> —*Give me the documents. I must hurry.*

He gave them to me, but whether or not they found the thief, I was not told. A big car, which I do not own, takes us to somewhere in Zagreb. We stop at an intersection because of my natural need. I then notice a large mass of people awaiting me, and as I spread my arms and raise them into the air, even my gesture helps everyone. I lie down and begin to read, when suddenly a bright light appears.

This is not a vision, but the actual physical world. And then with my physical eyes, I watch myself in that light. I am smiling broadly. Then, I become afraid because I notice that I have lost one of my front teeth. In that instant, the light vanishes and I see myself approaching myself. I am very afraid and scared that something might happen to me. At this point, the contact between the physical and the spiritual world is interrupted.

Then in a vision, I am in the village of my birth. I have nothing in common with the mass of people around me, and something prevents me from getting to my birth house. I take to the side streets and notice a pig of a hundred kilograms [220 lbs.] turning on a spit.

They explain to me:

—These are the provisions for your journey to Zagreb!

Passage is forbidden, everything is mined and I do not know where the land mines have been deployed. In the vision, I come across three male guards, with an acquaintance of mine among them. He laughs at me and yet lets me pass. I go further and arrive at an airport. I take off on a plane made of a completely unknown metal.

With me are many other passengers who also board the plane. By the way, during the flight, the rest of the passengers vanish. I remain alone in the cabin with my daughter. We travel to an unknown island, but end up landing in Krk. At the Krk airport, I come to know that two rulers will meet on that other island and divide the world between themselves. I do not know which island this is and what it looks like. I have not been told. My travels still had not resumed, because we would have needed to take a boat to get to the other island, which I did not want to do.

I am traveling again, this time by car. We arrive at the Hungarian border. I cannot pass through, therefore, I must return back to Zagreb. I suddenly see a basket I have seen before in earlier visions, connected to my astral journeys into the underworld. It is full of objects. At the crossroads, there are three men. They stop and inform me:

—*Last night, when you were travelling, the post office was broken into. Should you wish to pass, you must pay.*

—*But, I did not do this!*

—*We know, but it must be paid.*

—*Alright then, I will pay.*

In the vision, it was as if the payment was complete, at that very moment. I wish to continue my journey, but I cannot.

—*You still cannot go where you want to go. You do not have a passport!*

—*I have it at home!*

116

In that moment, the way opened and I received a permit to pass.

VISION:

In 1990, in a vision that I personally consider significant, a Herzegovinian man and I were together in the house. We were told:

> *—A decisive night lies in front of you! You are both powerful, but whichever one of you falls asleep will sleep until the end of the age. The other, who is awake, will be the chosen one.*

We talked and talked and the Herzegovinian suddenly grew weary and fell asleep. I won.

I went out of my house and heard a voice informing me that I have now opened three doors. I looked around and indeed saw doors in the house, three exits. I let the tap water run.

I was told:

> *—No one will be able to wake him and his lineage.*

That same year of 1990, a vision again took me to the hospital, and again I encountered the same Herzegovinian. He asked for forgiveness. He incidentally also threatened:

> *—If I had not given you that land, you could not be the person you are. Help me. If you do not help me, I will return to the land and destroy you!*

I replied:

—*You are forgiven.*

He left, pleased.

A year later, in a vision, I was in a cornfield, harvesting corn to feed the chickens. Suddenly, I noticed two men approaching me. One of them was that Herzegovinian. The other one was some Bosnian man. I hid so they would not notice me. They were arm in arm, like brothers. A while later, I astral traveled to my home and came by the Herzegovinian again. We were building a small wall in the attic of the house. He was smaller than a poppy seed and completely subservient to me.

I am then told that I have to leave immediately. So I rush and when I arrive, I am presented with a horse chained in gold. I ride him and in my hands carry a spiked club. I face a walled path, which I break through and open with the horse.

Then, the Serbian army pours in, but I beat them. I return back as a victor. In the meantime, the Herzegovinian has completely finished the building work started in my house.

I am pleased.

At this point, the vision promptly ceases and I am again in the physical world. This next vision is also tied to the Herzegovinian. Together we came to a shepherd herding a flock of sheep encircled in a wall. I tell him:

> —*Sir, you will not keep and preserve this wall for long. Come on, let the sheep loose.*

The shepherd replied:

—I will give you twenty of them, no more.

Together, we approached the doors in the wall, and my son suddenly came. He stood by the doors in order to count the sheep set loose for me. But then, an old woman materialized, a Serbian, and went after Alen with pitchforks. She wanted to stab him. The Herzegovinian and I intervened and drove her away.

Then, the shepherd said:

—When someone scolds your son in justice, punish him with love, not a beating!

In one of my earlier visions, when I was buying that house, there was a little pile of white beans on the table. Out of that small heap, suddenly, a huge pile was created. There was so much of it to eat that it could never be finished. I kept feeding more and more people with these beans. Suddenly, I was carried over to a football stadium. I was a waiter. And again, I was feeding people.

But this did not last for long.

I travelled astrally to a wasteland, where there was a kiosk full of clothes. There was no salesman in the kiosk. There were also no shoppers. I flew further with my Spirit guide and saw a forest, with a woman in it. She gave me a basketful of plumbs.

I raced on and found myself in Zagreb, in the outskirts of the city. Here, a brook flowed that stank and people were throwing shoes into it. The woman who owned all those shoes was in Germany. I felt sorry that other people's goods were being destroyed.

Along with the shoes, people were also throwing clothes into the foul smelling brook. The polluted brown water flowed over it all and washed it away. There were some individuals who snatched the clothes to steal it, taking it away.

I interfered in this pillage, but only managed to save two dolls for the owner. Everything else was snatched up by the masses, or perished in the bilge water.

Who knows what more would have happened, for at this point, I heard a voice announce:

—*The one in the Great Gorica is sentenced to 540 human years of punishment!*

Who this referred to was not revealed to me. As soon as I heard the imposed sentence, I immediately left everything behind and no longer wanted to interfere in the pillage.

The announcements of what I saw in my visions during the year of 1990 are especially significant for me.

VISION:

I was in Serbia, in a meadow. A shining cross came down from the sky. With it came a dome that had six compartments, and bees were flying out of them in all directions. In their flight, they grew more distant from the dome. A plane stood nearby. A Serbian man got into it and flew off towards the West.

VISION:

I was working as a fish seller in a fish market in a town that was completely unfamiliar to me. This was like another vision from a day in 1989. Fog was descending and some people showed me something that was in the haze. Then, they threw it and I caught it. As I caught it, the fog grew even more dense and opaque. I walked through this fog, and found that I had strayed and was lost. I cried out:

—*Dear God, where am I?*

A light began shining and revealed the path I had been taking. After a while, I found myself in front of a small house where there were people.

They said:

—*Here he is, he has returned! Where have you been?*

I admitted:

—*I do not know, I could not see anything in the fog, and the light brought me to you!*

And then the vision ceased.

VISION:

Even today I recall a particularly impressive vision that I had on December 23, 1972. I saw myself in a factory, which I later recognized as OKI, even though in reality of the physical world, I do not know if the OKI existed as early as 1972, let alone how it may have looked. Inside of the factory, between the entrance and the operations facility, I saw a great mill grinding wheat.

I was told:

> —*You see, now your wheat is being ground, your pictures. They will accuse you, condemn and slander you for 15 earthly months. You shall be accused of thievery, and your picture will even appear in the newspaper!*

I was ashamed.

Shortly afterwards, I was brought to a train rushing through the darkness. It sped by so quickly that nothing could be seen out of the windows. The train was racing so fast that I was afraid it might derail at a turn.

Cautiously, I asked a passenger:

> —*Where are we travelling?*

He mysteriously replied:

> —*You'll see.*

Finally, in the early dawn we arrived in Kruševac, a place I have never been to before. I got out, and nearby there was a market. I went over and looked around at the goods sitting out. At one bench, I decided to buy a bottle of oil and a small container, but could not because I did not have enough money.

Then I was told:

—There will come a time when you will be able to buy all of this. At that time, there will be a period of great famine!

—Why? I marveled deeply.

—War will erupt, brother against brother. This will be in the year that you redeem all these objects!

The vision disappeared and everything actually came true. Even though this vision is 20 years old, I have never spoken about it to anyone for fear of getting hurt. Now, this is the first time I am making it public.

There will be those who will reproach me for how easy it is to be a prophet, seeing an event that will happen, when such a prophecy has not been recorded anywhere. I am only left to swear that this prophecy was indeed communicated to me in a vision I had in 1972.

Why would I lie?

VISION:

The vision I am referring to happened in 1987. I was in the vineyards in Bagrem, a place unknown to me.

I was told:

—There is a ship that was placed in this location 7,500 human years ago. It is dead, but will come back to life in May 1992.

I was permitted to enter the ship and look around. There was a house on the deck. It was then said:

—*It stands here to cleanse the sea!*

I saw an old woman rushing from the ship, and into the acacia grove, saying:

—*I will give you all of it, both the bees and the honey, and you defend them!*

I did not believe her telling me there was honey. I took a shovel and began digging around the house. While digging, I indeed found honey. There were tons and tons of it. I covered it with clothes, not wanting other people to find it. I did not do this out of selfishness, but out of a desire to preserve and share it. Indeed, I was soon giving out honey to children and adults, and to each as much as they wanted and needed. Also, with me was that Herzegovinian, and I decided to live in the house on that ship forever.

VISION:

In 1992, I had this vision. For punishment, I had to serve as a gardener. I served for a long time, and then I was called into the house. A young man came to replace me at work. I was released, but before going, I had to teach him the job. We both took gardening shears. I was going to show him how to trim and shape the hedge. A bee flew passing by us. I caught it.

She said:

—*Do you see those four cherry trees? I planted them myself.*

124

I looked at the cherry trees and the fruit hung like grape bunches on them, with the branches almost breaking from the massive quantity of fruit. We marveled at this. Afterwards, I showed the young man how to trim the hedges and was happy to be leaving.

VISION:

One day, in 1990, my Spirit guide led me to Zagreb's Tuškanac Street. I was again held captive, but this time in an underground basement in solitary confinement, without any food or water. I was held captive by some woman.

I was told:

> —*Beware, when a black woman appears, the door of the cell will open. You will be able to get out, but do not exit to freedom through the door, but though the window!*

The guard was a quiet woman who was smoking all the time, and kept an eye on me so I could not attempt to escape. And then I clearly saw a black-haired girl approaching. There was not any way that the woman guard could prevent her from rescuing me.

I was free, but in the meantime, the black-haired woman began to go to sleep, and I also found it difficult to walk. Somehow, I knew that she did not realize whom she had freed, because I had secret powers that she was not aware of. I was told that she would be my companion for as long as she slept, for such was the force upon her.

When we reached a bridge, we were supposed to cross it together, but then we parted. She followed the path to the East. I kept an eye on her while she was crossing another bridge, and then I left. I knew she would wake up only when she reached the East.

VISION:

I was given to see an unusual white flower. From it curling upward came a heavy, luscious scent that was completely unknown to me. I instantly became aware that this scent does not exist today.

It was revealed to me that this scent, in the new civilization that comes, gives people eternal youth. With this scent, old age will be postponed, and the new civilization will present a new time.

VISION:

One of the more recent visions is completely incomprehensible and inexplicable to me, and it does not even lead me to any attempt at interpretation. Namely, I was on an astral journey, but together with my son Alen. I saw a clover on a hill and picked it.

MANIFESTATIONS

When I think hard, I have often experienced manifestations, but as hints to something more: I did not know how to interpret them.

For instance, in my house on Retkokac Street, I experienced a strange vision back in 1981. Immediately after I went to bed, I heard footsteps approaching my house. Then, I heard a knock and

I got up and opened the door. In front of me stood an unknown young man, about 20 years old, in a green velvet coat. Although his footsteps echoed loudly, the young man had no legs.

And all of a sudden, he disappeared.

I ran over to my neighbors, and told them that I saw someone at my door. We called out, searching for him, ran all around, but failed to make contact with this creature.

Anxious and shivering with discomfort, I returned to bed. At around 12:35 a.m., there was someone at the door once again. I got up thinking that the young man had returned.

When I opened the door, there was a turkey on the doorstep. I wanted him to come into the house, but just as I took him in my hands, he vanished. Frightened, I returned to bed but stayed awake, fearing more would happen next.

At 1:35 a.m., for the third time, I heard some banging. It was the sound of apples falling onto the house. It was an apple shower that drummed the tiles of the roof. There were so many of them that they could have covered the entire house with me in it. But, when I got up to see those apples that showered down on my house, there was no trace of them!

This was the time when everyone was envious of the things I had. The neighbors were talking behind my back:

—*He walks down the street throwing rocks, and money falls down on him!*

Whatever I would wish for would come true. But naturally, this could not last forever. I lost my job and poverty was knocking on the door. I didn't even have any wood to start a fire, so I secretly snuck into the nearby forest to collect some dry branches. There was not even a penny in the house.

Two years passed by like this without money for basic needs. I was not even able to buy potatoes. I could have become a crook, but since I never was one, I would never choose to be one, so I was simply helpless. I could not make any money with honest work, and did not want it in an indecent way.

And then, one evening, I was standing on the balcony of my house, and from my physical body, a light came out, which started dancing in front of my eyes like a firefly. When it began to move away, I rushed after it driven by a strange compulsion. That light led me into the fields, toward the river Sava, about four kilometers away from my home. All this happened in the middle of November. Hurrying after this firefly shining in the darkness, I came to a field. In it there were over 500 sacks of stacked potatoes!

I cried from happiness. I did not give into greed; I took ten sacks, so I could provide food for myself, my family and the pigs I was raising. And then that light, in the form of a firefly, went out and disappeared. I realized then how God had not abandoned me, but had instead given me a lesson in patience.

One should not believe that the treasure will last forever. That same winter, not even two months had passed from this event, when I had to take a bag into the forest to gather dry leaves and leftovers from the fields to feed the rabbits. I did not have any money. Again, I went at night, secretly, so the neighbors would not see me. I was ashamed of my poverty. My dog ran along behind me. When we were close to the forest, he paused, staring intently into the darkness beneath some bush. Then he ran up and began to nuzzle there. I curiously went after him.

Once there, I came across a beautiful light that was igniting on and off. I was scared, so I turned and ran. Then I heard a voice that calmed me down, telling me there was nothing to fear. It told me to go back. The voice was so persuasive that I listened to it. Despite still feeling afraid, I returned to that spot. Something appeared to me then. It was a human shape. I am sure of it! But, what exactly it was, to this day, I still do not know.

One Friday, I was getting ready for my usual work, selling fish. It was 5:15 a.m. on October 14, when I left my house. A few meters from my door, I saw a man who I had never seen before. He had a cigarette in his mouth and a newspaper under his right arm. He just stood there and I bristled while passing by him.

Given that the place where he was standing was not lit, I became curious and wanted to find out who this man was with the newspaper under his arm waiting for someone. So, I stopped waiting for my neighbor, so we could go on the bus together. But, when I turned around, to my great astonishment, that man with the newspaper and the cigarette was no longer there.

I asked my neighbor:

—*Please, tell me, where did that man go?*

The neighbor laughed at me and said I should stop hallucinating. He did not see any man and thought that I was probably still asleep.

I did not want to quarrel more with my neighbor, so I stood

quietly waiting for the bus to arrive, which took me to the tram station where I boarded the tram to go to Utrine Street. When I got off at the great crossroads of Držićeva and Vukovarska Avenues, I saw the same man again. He was just standing, holding the newspaper under his arm. I walked past him and then turned, but he was gone.

As I was changing to a tram for Zaprude Street, I felt uncomfortable and decided not to think about it. From Zaprude to Utrine, I went on foot. At the traffic lights near the fish market, my unknown companion appeared for the third time.

This time, he held the newspaper open to read, and the cigarette in his mouth was unlit. I eyed him, from head to toe, and stood next to him, waiting to see what would happen. Something most extraordinary, something utterly inexplicable, happened. As if, in a puff of smoke, that man suddenly disappeared.

I was particularly happy that day at work. I successfully sold fish like never before in my life, completely selling it all. Only later, did I discover who this was visiting me that morning.

It was the spirit of the man who would publish my first book.

THE SECRET KNOWLEDGE

The astral journeys of my consciousness outside my physical body have enabled me to realize some truths, which are not known to others. These, I have been given to pass on entirely or partially to everyone, so that people can protect themselves. It is so they know more about the world that they cannot see, which has a major influence on their lives and destinies.

One of my astral journeys took me into the underworld, and no one living has ever been allowed to do this before me. The journey began in a big black car, in the company of two women who were unfamiliar to me. We were on the way to Cazin to visit Tala, a Muslim, who claimed to have had close encounters with God.

On the highway from Zagreb to Karlovac Road, a strip of light came out of me during the drive. Actually, a piece of me fell out, which was shining very brightly. This was a piece of my Strength or Spirit guide, which had materialized. It fell into a pond of stagnant water by the road, under an apple tree with red fruit. Having fallen into this small pool, it started sinking to the bottom, and then through it, sinking deeper into the earth.

In some strange way, it pulled me along with it. After falling some forty meters, which was like descending down through the walls of a well, we touched upon solid ground. Then, I grabbed that shining part of myself with my right hand, and it said to me:

>—*The ruler of the underground world is here. Beware, if they see you, you will never get away!*

I looked around me and saw immense luxury with men and women enjoying themselves in orgies; it was a debauchery like I had never seen before.

Some shadows began approaching us and that piece of light quickly said to me:

>—*Run! Run away from here as quickly as possible! You are now the only one who knows about the entrance to the underground*

world! There will be great difficulties before you manage to get out of here, for dark has fallen, but do not forget that you will be saved as soon as the new day breaks!

Somehow, I managed to get out of the underground world. I found myself on the surface of the earth, but the car with those two unknown women was no longer there. I began walking to Cazin. That light, which had fallen out of my body earlier, continued to float by me. That materialized part of my Spirit guide constantly warned me to be careful.

Then, a young man on a motorbike approached me on the highway. My Spirit guide whispered:

—Run down the old Karlovac road! These are the spies of the underground world! They will take you back into the underworld! Fight!

The stranger on the motorbike quickly caught up with me and offered me a ride. As soon as I sat on the bike, I knew my Spirit guide was telling the truth and that the stranger was indeed a spy of the underworld conspirators. I boldly said this to his face. He did not deny it. He informed me that he needed to take me back as a prisoner.

I threw back the reply:

—You will never succeed!

Then, lights started turning on in the windows of the nearby houses. As people began waking up to see what was happening, I took advantage of the stranger's confusion and fled. I ran until I came across the milkmaid's house, Barice, asking her to give me shelter until daybreak. She could not understand why I was running and hiding. I tried to explain:

—Because I am the only one on the earth who knows the entrance into the underground world. But there will come a time when the massacre of people and its victims across the country passes, and then I will be able to publicly speak. For on that day, in the daylight, none of the underground spies will have any power!

The stranger on the bike found me likeable and inadvertently took my side. He confided that he would spare me. He was then not able to return to the underworld, but after him, millions would come who would not let me go. And so it was.

I did not stay for long at the home of the milkmaid Barica, because evil forces were constantly attacking. I crept surreptitiously in the dark since the Sun had not yet risen. I left, and it was just at the time of some carnival festivities. I took advantage of the crowds, ran, got away and hid in a tavern. I hid among the bottles, for all around it was crawling with underground spies.

They were looking for me but were unable to find me. Then, a train set off and they followed after it. The train was on its way to Serbia! I came out of my hiding place among the bottles in the tavern, and saw a bicycle. When I recognized it as the one I actually have in physical life, I sat on it and rushed away.

Where to? I did not know.

After some time, I noticed a tall, blond man behind me. I do not know how, but I recognized him and knew who he was. He was carrying a basket.

He approached me and said:

> —*Do not be afraid! We have been watching it all, but none of us were allowed to assist you; you had to get out of the danger on your own. You are going to help people and heal them. Once the basket is full of inscriptions, which you will give to people, then hand it over to those above!*

A bright light was shining from the basket. I realized I was on the path of truth.

I continued on my way.

Before the morning came, for all this happened just before dawn, the daylight to come would just not break! I arrived at an unfamiliar place and again went into a tavern where there were many people, all tired, hung over and sleepy, and my sister was among them. I wanted to tell her everything, and I also wanted to inform the police about the entrance into the underground world, but none of these tired people would listen to me. I could only manage to find out the name of the town.

It was called Deligrad.

They said there was still another hour until dawn. It would take me that much time to get to my childhood home where I wanted to go. Here, I thought the people would understand me, and I would be able to confide my great secret to them.

Today, I know that I have arrived at the symbol of the house, after 42 months, in February 1992. Now it has finally dawned, and I may openly tell everyone everything.

CHAPTER 5

A HEALER'S PATH

TOUCH A MAN AND HE WILL HEAL

In May 1990, I was asleep and while sleeping a vision appeared to me, and with spirit I left my physical body.

An unknown, dark-skinned man took me into the forest behind my house and explained that there was elm wood in it, and he showed me how I should break off a twig and use it for healing. When I explained what had happened to me during this event to other people, some of them advised me to stay silent about it, while others told me I was insane. So, no one would believe me.

Still, when I told one friend of mine about my visions, she just said:

—*Touch a man and he will heal!*

To my surprise, she told me that thirty years ago, a man who was one of Zagreb's most famous fortunetellers using coffee grounds, had informed her that one day a man would knock on her door whose touch would make people feel better.

Then she went on:

> —*There will be people who will come and they will change all of this, and you will be able to speak of this publicly, clearly and loudly. Everyone will believe you, apart from your enemies and your wife, Mara. They will be the last to start believing, but once they do, they will believe more than everyone else. When you are ridiculed, do not be afraid. The masses will keep you safe.*

She advised me not to talk to anyone, because the authorities that opposed healing could have me arrested. That would ruin me. Thus, I did not speak to anyone about this and continued working at the fish market until further notice came.

Again, there was an unknown woman who announced to me:

> —*Ivica, the power is yours and it will come to you!*

I found myself above the bed, seeing myself floating in spirit above my physical body, which was deep in slumber below in the bed. With my spiritual body I reunited with my physical one through the rib. At that moment, I opened my eyes and was back in my physical, earthly life.

Since that night, I have felt a sweet current in my body, and with my palms, I have touched the sick that came to me seeking my help. And, they have healed regardless of their prior conditions.

THE POWER IS YOURS

On Sunday, immediately after this event, I found out that some people were healing using bioenergetics at the "Hotel I" in Zagreb. I called them and arranged a visit on Tuesday. Here, I met a woman and a younger male.

At first they would not admit me to their healing sessions because they were over-booked. But, I kept insisting and the woman finally took me in as a patient. She had me lay face down on the bed.

I closed my eyes. I did not know what she was doing to my body. Then, all of a sudden, I heard a voice:

—Look who came to us!

Thinking that someone had quietly entered the room, and she was talking about them, I did not pay any attention to her words.

Then, I heard her voice again:

—Sir, we are very small in comparison to you! You are the one who should be helping people!

She shook me and I realized that she was actually talking to me all along. I was dumbfounded when they said they could not help me. I begged and implored them, but they kept making gestures with their fingers of how small they were in relation to me. This, I could not understand at all. Here I was sick, and they were claiming that I should actually be the one helping other people!

In the end, I finally managed to convince them to resume my

bioenergetic treatment. I came to them five times, and felt no improvement. But, when I came the sixth time, something unusual happened. I left my house in the pouring rain. Everyone had umbrellas that were barely protecting them from the downpour, but I did not have one.

However, by some miracle, not a single drop of rain fell on me!

I entered the "Hotel I" with my clothes completely dry. When they saw me entering the room without an umbrella, they asked me:

—*Did you come by taxi?*

—*No, I came on a tram and then by foot*, I answered.

They just looked at one another mutely.

—*What is it?* I asked wondering.

But there was no reply.

They had me lie down on the bed and put their palms on my stomach, heart and head. Suddenly, something started happening.

I had a vision!

No matter how unbelievable the following lines might sound, this is exactly how it all happened:

Big, thick black smoke started coming out of me, and I could discern a threatening wolf exposed in it.

Then, in the smoke, six harnessed black horses appeared, pulling an old fashioned carriage with my grandfather sitting on the seat within. The trotting horses pulled the carriage on a journey to the West. As soon as the carriage dashed off, my body was engulfed in a fever.

I shook all over.

And then, instead of the thick, black smoke, bluish-green smoke started coming out of me. I could feel the aura around my body expanding and filling, and I grew hotter. I saw a fog, and through it was the rise of the first morning sun. As the dawn was established, everything around me instantly became clear and pure. From the sun, a procession of children, women, friends, familiar and unfamiliar people, started coming out followed by children with golden wings. I was shown six thick golden chains and then a seventh, the thickest one of them all.

The bioenergetic healers interrupted my vision and brought my spirit back into my physical body. They told me:

>—*Now you are cured. You have the strongest aura in Croatia, and you may do anything you wish.*

The man then added:

>—*You see all and can do anything you like, but be careful and do not abuse what you have been given. Do as your heart tells you. The power is yours!*

GUIDE WITH THE SUN

Completely confused, I went home. It was an extraordinary day. Whatever I wanted to see that day, past, future, friends or enemies, everything, and I mean absolutely everything, I actually saw all day long.

But, when I came home and went into the bedroom, something leapt upon me. Some force grabbed onto me and I completely froze up. I could not even move.

I was like this for three days.

I lay motionless on the bed and then on the third day, through the window, I saw a young man who was at the time 16 years old. He was walking down the street. There was a light shining above his head, and inside of me, I heard a voice telling me to call him over and to pay him as much as he wanted for giving me a good massage.

When I called him, I was surprised because he accepted without any hesitation, as if he expected it.

He massaged me for a long time, until at one point he cried out:

> —*Ivica, there are three colors on your body! Green, blue and yellow!*

I did not believe him so we called in my daughter, Marijana. She also saw those colors that appeared on my skin. I asked them to pass me a mirror to see it for myself. And indeed, I could clearly see those three colors on my back.

With great effort, I dragged myself to the bathroom to take a shower after the massage. I locked the door and lay in the bathtub.

I screamed.

I saw a man falling from the cross. He was still hanging by a nail through his right hand, but he was nevertheless falling! He jerked his hand and he fell off the cross, which separated from his body.

Then, the cross flew in the air and fell on my forehead. Ever since that day, I have a scar on my forehead in the shape of a cross.

I was screaming in terror. When the young man broke open the door, he saw me in the bathtub.

Blood was shooting from my palms.

Since then, I have a pronounced healing power. I would touch anyone in pain with my hands, and in that moment they would heal and the pain would disappear.

This was confirmed on January 19, 1992, when a new vision appeared to me. It took me to the house of my birth, and to the same bed where I once lay.

I am sitting and listening to the following words:

—*Son, you have 75 grams of gold on you. When you have a kilogram, you will be a direct guide with the Sun. Go to "Hotel I" to your teacher for some instructions on how you will continue to work.*

Immediately, by the very next day, this man from the "Hotel I" started sending me sick people, whom I have successfully helped. The first among them was Mrs. Razija Grgić, and she was followed by many others.

THE FIRST HEALING

Again it was Friday, and I was selling fish. When I looked up, standing right there amongst the people was a woman, and I saw light atop her head.

I walked over to her and asked:

>—*Madam, are you Razija Grgić?*

She said:

>—*I am, that's me. What do you need?*

To this I replied:

>—*You are not looking for fish, you were sent to find me to help you.*

She was amazed and said:

>—*Yes, I'm waiting for you if you're the Ivica they call Gypo. I was sent from "Hotel I" because they cannot help me. But, you will help me.*

So it started. Razija received the help for which she came. Today, she is cured, a happy woman who is very grateful to me.

I will always endeavor to help people. As I did then, so I do now. When you come to me, with your very arrival, you are irradiated and have already received help. How I do it, judge for yourself.

And now a lot of love to You, and as you read my words, learn from me. I sincerely love you all very much, and all the things I have written, these are the visions given to me that I convey and pass on to you.

Follow them together with me. That time is coming, let us rejoice, and let us receive the happiness and joy that await us.

I HAVE HELPED THEM

I will have to give a word from the people who have been coming to see me. Here, I am mindful of the many thousands of patients who have requested my help, which they have received. I will speak about them in this book, because they wish to be a part of alternative healing history. Due to limited space in this book, I am unable to describe everyone I have helped, but will outline the most difficult cases, which speak for themselves. Deservedly, I begin with Mrs. Razija Grgić, as she was among the first who came seeking my help.

Razija Grgić

I was really sick, and had been ill for many years. I visited many medical institutions, seeking a cure from everyone, but no one was able to help me. I was very nervous, and I received injections of tranquilizers. Aside from that, I was also suffering from a sense of asphyxiation in my chest, which also spread to my neck. Everything hurt. I was not only seeking help from doctors, but also from herbalists and bioenergy practitioners. I lost all hope of being healed and I did not believe that anyone existed who could help me or give me any hope for a brighter future. Who could help me to heal, so that one day, I would be happy in my life? My savior, if I may call him this, is called Ivica. I went to him for sessions and now you can see the changes. I am a healthy and happy woman, I feel very, very good. I am grateful to Mr. Ivica, and not only for me, but for everyone; my husband, my children, my many friends who knew about the pain I had within me for so many years, and for all I know.

Even if I gave him all the wealth in this world, I could not repay him enough for what he has done for me, eternal thanks.

Drago Marić

I was suffering from neurosis and I constantly had pressure in my chest. I was treated by many doctors and herbalists, but there was no cure for me. Since I was a regular reader of the magazine *Vikend*, I read an article in which Mrs. Razija Grgić wrote about her problems and how Ivica from Zagreb healed her. I immediately went to him. He then examined me and recognized the illness that caused my suffering. I did everything as Sir advised. Today, I am a married man, and I no longer have the neuroses, and I do not visit doctors. And look now, two months ago I had a son. I thank our dear Sir for he helped me greatly, and now I am a happy father and a happy man.

Marijana Stipčić

I first came to Ivica because of love problems, which I was unable to resolve myself. He just looked in the mirror and told me:

—*My dear Marijana, black magic has been cast upon you.*

I was also sure of this deep down inside. He even found out who did this. He spoke as if he had known me forever, even though until that moment, he had never seen me before. What else could I do but believe him. At that moment for me, something amazing happened, and it was as if someone took a huge burden off my shoulders and soul. I came to Ivica several times after that. I will not say that I am married with a happy marriage already. I am still very young, but what I had inside of me is gone.

I am calmer now, thanks to our Sir, and I have found myself a boyfriend, who will probably be my future husband. Once again, I thank Mr. Ivica very much.

Sladan Dušanić

As everyone else, I have come to put on record in this book my words of love for our great Sir. I was nervous at the time when I first met our Sir; I would withdraw into myself, insecure, timid, and afraid of people. After his treatments and our conversations, I acquired my spiritual peace. I came to know my own values and myself. My nervousness has disappeared, I have been reborn and now experience great well being. Luck has returned to my home. I have become a completely different man, and there is nothing I can wish but for our Sir to continue helping many other people as he has helped me.

Much thanks to him, and whomever reads this, may you understand that spiritual peace is the greatest treasure in the world. Thank you.

Sandra Razić

The first time I came to Ivica was in May 1991, and regardless of how many people were there, I immediately thought that this man would help me. I waited impatiently and did not want to talk to anyone about my troubles. Everyone was quiet and waiting for our Sir to appear at the door. When he appeared, I was expecting an old man, however, in front of me appeared a dynamic man, full of charm, strictly professional, smiling and saying:

>—*You, woman, you want me to say your name.*

I looked at him and he said:

>—*It is written on your forehead that your name is Sandra, come in.*

I came in and sat down on the chair, and you would not believe me, but I began to tremble with some sort of excitement. He wrote down my name and looked at the lit candle's flame, then to his old mirror and started talking to me.

>—*My Sandra, why do you act so frightened when luck is knocking on your door? You are married, you have everything, but you do not have children. But, you will bear a child so lively and playful, like my Alen, and this, my dear sister, is what a brother wishes for you. You have been under a spell to this day, and this has been going on for no less than 12 years.*

146

When the man told me that I was married for 13 years, and said all that, I said to myself, well, if he doesn't help me have a baby. This was just a thought, I didn't say anything out loud, and our Sir replied jokingly:

—For heaven's sake, woman, I'm not going to make you a baby. You have a husband at home for that, he will make you give birth.

I was really shivering, as some sweet current went through me, and he said:

—Woman, a blessing is upon you.

He described everything nicely to me and said:

—You will be a mother in nine months.

When I got home, I told my husband everything, word for word, since we were in an ideal marriage. My husband believed it all so much that he also wanted to meet Ivica. And, that is what he did. And truly, after 9 months, I gave birth to a son and named him Alen. As the Sir said, so the child was born.

There is no money in the world or wealth that could pay for this. Please understand, he would not take anything, he only said:

—Spread the word, woman, and say thank you.

That is all I have ever given to our Sir.

Damijan Mitrović

I came to the gentleman in October 1991, on 28 Tuškanova Street. When I came, he immediately said to me:

—Why do you seek someone deceased, do you want me to return him to you?

I just looked at the gentleman and confirmed that this was so. He started talking and no one apart from me could know about the many things that he said. What else can I say; he had it all right. So, he told me we would try but did not promise anything, he just said:

—Mr. Mitrović, we shall try. If it succeeds, you can only thank God, not me.

I will mention that I was financially broke at the time. When it was over, I was meaning to ask how much this all cost. To my great surprise, he beat me to it and said:

—But you don't have a penny in your pocket, how would you pay me? You are not even fully aware of where you have come!

He told me to come back again for treatment. As I didn't have any money, I was very embarrassed to be in front of this man. I was not able to come back again, since this man cannot be lied to.

But, no matter how insistent I was that I would no longer like to visit our Sir, there was an invisible force pulling me back again. To my great surprise, in the room where he worked, there was an unknown woman about 60 years old. She just looked at me and said to our Sir:

—Ivica, I shall tell you something. This man will come to you, I saw him in March of this year. This is the man, remember, he will work for you.

Once more I was shocked, and asked myself how I could work for this gentlemen and why me. I did not contradict this then, since I had been rejected for work everywhere. And then I resumed my treatments. I asked, when it was all over, how much is the cost, and our Sir smiled and said:

—Leave as much as you consider not too much, for your good luck. Now you have money on you.

I took out 500 Dinaris[1] and said it would stand for my good fortune. Well, this is all I have ever paid our gentleman. This is the only thing I left and it was really from my heart. I should mention that at the time, I was working as a craftsman on heavy masonry jobs and went on doing so until something began to happen to me and my feelings.

After some time, somewhere in the spring of the same year, I stopped by again to see our gentleman and brought him what I then considered to be a good gift, as a token of my appreciation to thank him. Then, I stopped by another time and as soon as I walked in, he asked me how I was doing. I answered that I was feeling good, thank God.

Our gentleman asked me:

---

[1] Hyperinflation took place during the Croatian War of Independence from 1991–1995, with one of the worse currency plummets in history. 500 Dinaris had a small relative value.

—Well, are you still in the construction business?

I replied affirmatively and he said:

> *—You know, sir, I have some work around the house to be done with construction materials, would you want to do this for me? I will pay you.*

We made an arrangement that I would come over, but I did not go there, I was prevented from doing so. I came home and went to bed. I do not know how you will believe me when I tell you what happened next. That same gentleman, believe it or not, was standing right in my house. He said:

> *—Why didn't you come? I was waiting for you.*

He continued:

> *—We helped you, so you come nicely to my office and do the job you promised. You will be blessed.*

I was trembling all over, and after he spoke those words, he disappeared. As suddenly as he appeared, he disappeared.

I should mention that I was not sleeping, I was lying down, but really only resting. I was scared and I would have gone to him that instant had I known where to go. I could not wait for the day to break to go and see our gentleman.

I came and wanted to tell him. He just laughed and said, as always:

> *—Mitrović, you must realize that there are no coincidences, that*

*everything is predetermined. So you have come here to do what
you have been predestined to do.*

I emphasize, I went and did the job. Upon completion of my
work, the gentleman organized a big celebration at his house, but
the waiter who was supposed to work did not show up. As I found
myself already there, what else could I do but offer my services to
do this work. My first task was to slice two goats and a suckling-
pig. Having done this, I was given the role of serving his guests. I
can tell you, it was the first time I found myself in a role that I
performed with my whole heart and soul. There were some
familiar people there, and one of them said:

—*He passed! It means Damijan can work for our Sir.*

Our gentleman responded:

—*Mitrović, be to work on Friday!*

I could not wait for September 18, 1992, to appear in the company
of our great gentleman. Since then and to this day, I have been
working for our gentleman. He pays me a salary and I am so
happy. Those who read this book; I have told this story to
everyone and I will continue to tell it for as long as I live. Not ever
in my entire life have I lived better than I do now. I should point
out that I only have an eighth grade education, and now I do the
work I never dreamed I would do. I am overjoyed that in my life,
as the gentleman says, a loving person is just about to come. I am
now 38 years old, and one day wish to get married and be happy.
This is the kind of happiness I wish for, and God willing, I will
have it. Thanks to God and to our gentleman.

Ana Milić

First, a big thanks to our Sir. Furthermore, I wish to present my case. I am 36 years old; I am a mother of two children and have a husband whom I love very much. My nightmares began no less than 10 years ago, immediately after I married my husband. My husband is of the Muslim faith, so I married him out of love, because we were very, very much in love. I could never please my mother-in-law and his family, not even today. They did not accept me because I am a Catholic, and they are Muslims. This is as much as I can say about myself and now I will begin my story of how I came to our Sir.

What I have said was an introduction, just so you know that I was in such great torment and in difficult life endangerment.

At the time, my right kidney failed and I needed 50,000 German Marks for an operation in Germany. I would also have consented to the surgery, if I had not come to our dear Sir at the time.

If you ask me how I came to him, believe me, it was very difficult, as I stated already, so bear with me. When I found out about this gentleman, Ivica, at 28 Tuškanova Street, I immediately set out to see him on June 29, 1992.

As I had nowhere to leave my girls, I had to bring them along with me. I realized that many people come and so I thought that having my kids with me would make it easier for me to get through the long line more quickly. To my great surprise, I was immediately disappointed. The trick did not work. When I rang the bell, a man with black hair appeared and said from the balcony:

—Who do you need?

I said:

—Sir, if you are Mr. Ivica, I need you.

He immediately told me:

—Woman, I do not admit children!

This devastated me. Nothing else was left but to plead. When I saw that my requests were not helping, the man said:

—Woman, if you understand Croatian, I do not admit children up here!

I did not understand this. Moping, I returned home and immediately called my friend Dragica, and told her that he would not admit me.

And then she replied:

—Well, why didn't you say that I sent you?

—Oh, I did say all this, but he said that he does not admit people with children.

She explained:

—Well, yes. Sir does not admit children, because he sees many people meeting at his place and black magic comes out of them, and so a child might be affected by this black magic. That's why he also doesn't want children coming to him. He works one day a month with children only, and not adults.

I immediately felt liberated. I did not dare go to our Sir again. I must confess; I started to fear him. But I have to also confess that an invisible energy was leading me back to our Sir. I had to come again and Mrs. Dragica took me.

When I walked in and sat down on the chair, I admit that I immediately felt a tingling throughout my entire body. On the spot where I had great pain in my right kidney, I felt such sweetness, as if I was having one orgasm after another. I knew something was going on, which I cannot even explain today. I should point out that I was ready for surgery. When I went to see my doctor afterwards, all the doctors were truly perplexed.

They asked where my condition had gone, and I said:

—*To Tuškanova Street, with Mr. Ivica.*

He told me that I had two young daughters, and a husband of a different religion, and he could not have known this earlier. He further told me that my husband's parents cannot stand me, and that his entire family would never accept me, but that my husband and I are destined for each other. He said he could see my husband's path in Italy. Bear in mind that my husband is still in Italy even today. At the time, we could never have dreamed this was possible, but as you can see, all has come true, and all the spells have vanished. My kidney is now working as it should, and this is documented. I did not need to have surgery and I am a happy and healthy woman. With this, I thank my, and our, dear Sir. Were I to give him all the treasure in this world, he would still not be paid or repaid. My children are happy today, as is my husband, and again, great thanks to Mr. Ivica.

Mrs. Jagica

I came to Sir on July 14, 1990. Bear in mind that I had already been declared blind, and I was carrying a blind person's cane and could not see that man at all. When they brought me in, I was rheumatic all over.

Upon entering his office, I immediately felt positive radiation and said to myself:

—This is where I will get help.

I emphasize that I could barely walk and was blind, and the Sir asked me:

—Grandma, how old are you?

I said I was 56, to which he laughed and said openly that I looked like I was 76 years old, and continued:

—Mother, I am not God, so I cannot bring you back your sight and make you younger.

I must admit that I greatly implored him to try, even if he could not heal me. He said:

—Very well, we shall try, but don't blame me if we do not succeed.

I was with him on Friday, and by Monday my situation had improved so very much that I no longer had to carry my cane. I was walking with the help of my friends, and came to our Sir once again. I should point out that I am not from Zagreb, I am from

Sisak, and I always had to take the train to go for a treatment. When he saw me on Monday, he said to me:

—*Well, you're no longer using the cane; apparently you've grown younger.*

I told him how I had dreamt of some church, and a man was in that church with his arms outstretched, standing and killing two snakes. Once he had killed both snakes, the man spoke to me and said:

—*Jagića, come, we shall nevertheless succeed, you will see but only with one eye, the left one, we cannot bring back the right one, and tomorrow you will be able to walk on your own, without an aid.*

I also immediately told everyone in the house about this, and they said that we should give this man something, but we did not have any money. I said I would sell 200 kilograms of wheat, and go to this man for the sake of my health.

I visited Ivica six more times, and on Friday another miracle happened when I arrived to his office. I saw some rays of light with my left eye, as I had dreamt about earlier. In the meantime, a woman came in and while Sir was treating me, I heard her ask:

—*So, why are speaking that way to this woman, can she see?*

And he answered:

—*No, Raza, this is a blind person. She insistently claims that from my hands she will manage to see.*

When that woman stood in front of me, an even greater miracle occurred. As if through a thick fog, her form began appearing to me. I described how there was something shining on her head, it was her glasses, and this was where the ray of hope appeared that I would be able to see.

Our Sir began with the treatment and all of a sudden, what happened?! I saw his face. I told him what he looked like, and the color of his hair. I simply cannot describe how I felt at the time. There is nothing else to say but many thanks to our Sir. He has really helped me a lot, and I can genuinely see with my left eye and I can also read. Since then, I have continued to visit our Sir, and am so exceedingly glad that he helps other people.

Rifat Mujić

Quite by accident, I found out through the press that there was someone in Zagreb named Ivica, at 28 Tuškanova Street. As soon as I heard of this, I came. It was on September 1, 1992. He admitted me and asked:

—*Sonny, why have you come?*

From my pocket, I took a photo of my 13-month old son, who was suffering from a dangerous illness, leukemia, and was then in a hospital in Zagreb. I took the photo and said, help my child. The gentleman looked at me and said:

—*My son, but I am not God. How can I help your child suffering from a severe and serious illness?*

And I said:

—*You will help him, I believe in you.*

He took the photo of my child, and laid it on that old mirror. What he did and how he did it, I do not know, all I know is that when I came to the hospital later, the doctors said my child was getting better. When I came to Zagreb for the second time, and note that I am not from around here, I am from Osijek, all the swelling disappeared from the child. I immediately ran to our Sir, at Tuškanova Street, and said something was happening with my son.

He would irradiate me with his hands and at the same time, my child's condition would improve. When I went to the hospital, I would see the medical establishment completely baffled by my child's improvements.

I wanted to pass this on to the head doctor; that my child was actually being helped by a man, who was well known to us, had published a book, and this help was coming directly from him. The doctor looked at me, but did not comment on anything, and with every day that passed my child's condition improved. I should mention now that my son came out of the hospital, and is at home in Osijek. With this, I would like to advise all parents that faith is stronger than anything in this world, and that the success came from my having faith in this man. My child came back straight from the dead.

Dragica Kalčićek

On June 1, 1990, a middle-aged man named Ivica knocked on my door at Tuškanova Street. I must mention that doctor Branka, who is my son's doctor, brought him here and he asked me to allow him into my kitchen, which is nine square meters.

As we were very ill and in poor material standing, Mr. Ivica saw this and said:

>—*Yes, I will work in your kitchen. I get such signals, and now Dragica, what I tell you remember well. When it all comes true, then I will leave.*

On the first day, he only brought one patient and when the patient left, in the presence of a few witnesses, he said the following words to me:

>—*Dragica, you and I can never fall out.*

At the time, it was unclear what he meant.

>—*Between the two of us, there will be a lot of dread and nightmares, and we will come into conflict. But, there is a great fairy standing between us, keeping a watchful eye to make sure no major problems arise.*
>
>*I will stay here, Dragica, for 29 to 33 human months. Remember, a lot of people will start off here and miracles will occur right in this room, on this spot.*

He signaled the spot too. And at the time, I was staring at the man because I did not understand. At times I thought he was hallucinating and had a wild imagination.

He told me:

>—*Mrs. Dragica, watch out so that money does not put you in*

jeopardy. If you do not accept and do not give in to money, we will solve all the problems ourselves, without any nightmares.

Then he continued:

—Money, Dragica, is the biggest whore, and man is not aware of how much negative energy comes just through money. You see, I will never charge anyone, not one cent, and if the person has nothing, I will always present him with my work and my help regardless, without taking a single penny.

I have to say that even after 30 months, Ivica has not charged anyone. He remained the same as when he first came. All that he said to me then, I can freely testify to the fact that it all came true, right to the last letter, absolutely everything. Had I realized what he was saying to me at the time, my son would have healed long ago, but here I can say this was my own fault.

In this small confined space, there have been as many people as there are hairs on one's head, it has been uncountable. But, it all came true just as Ivica said. So many people would wait and everything happened so smoothly, as if there was not a single person in the room. Trust me, as you may know, it has always been full, but the divine presence is so strong that everyone is so happy just to be close to Mr. Ivica.

If I could describe it all, I would always describe it as miracles that only God can create. Ivica would only show up and point, and even greater peace would take over and all eyes would hold love for him. There is nothing too hard for me to do for these people. Whenever someone would come to my door, ring the bell, and ask for help from our Sir, I would receive such strength and always with a smile give the information of when our Sir is working, for how long, and when he is coming. There was never anything that was too hard to do for these people.

I fervently wish to thank our Sir publicly, whom not only I, but all those who turn to him, we all actually love him so very, very much and we all look to him with love. Thank you very much for everything that you did for us, for me and for my son, Željko. One only needs to trust and it all just comes true as he says it will.

Stojanka Dukić

I came to 28 Tuškanova Street. I must say that I was sent by one of my colleagues. At the time, I worked in an office and performed managerial tasks. I felt some discomfort and I had pressures coming from all sides. I suddenly began to fade, I mean like a snowdrop. There was so much turmoil in my house, and the spiritual world in my life and my home was all spellbound.

In February 1992, it was the hardest time for me, when my friend from work told me a story of visiting this Ivica at 28 Tuškanova Street. I did not believe in any magic, or alternatives, in nothing of the kind. I was raised in the spirit of communism and that is why I stated the functions I performed. I would never have thought of turning to such a person, as I actually did not know such people existed, because I was not interested.

In great disbelief, I still decided to go and visit Tuškanova Street and Mr. Ivica. Now, the miracles began to happen. When I entered the room, that is the small waiting room where Mr. Ivica works, I immediately felt different, and trust me, I was not even aware of where I found myself.

There were about ten people inside, and instantly a man appeared at the door, a man one is not lucky enough to meet every day, at least it seemed so to me. He walked with one patient, opened the door, and raised his hands. From those hands something shone so strongly, and he spoke gently and gracefully. I, and all those present, looked at him. To my great surprise, he gazed at us well and spoke my name.

—*Stojanka, you do not believe in me, why have you come?*

I am trembling now, let alone then; I began shaking like a leaf, becoming anxious and yet I was immersed in a kind state of well-being. With a quaking voice, I could hardly speak about never turning to such people as Mr. Ivica.

He smiled again and said:

—*I will admit you. Wait, when my angel marks you, I will receive you and you will get what you came for.*

I was received at about 11 o'clock. I stayed with Mr. Ivica for about half an hour, and at that time I became such a believer, as I remain to this day. The complete conversation happened in his office. First he told me that I was the mother of two.

I looked at him. I already doubted it all. I did not answer, I am the mother of one child.

As if he read my thoughts:

—*Yes, Stojanka, you gave birth to only one son, but you have raised this girl from a young age when her mother died. I told you this to tempt you to both believe and disbelieve in me.*

Then I nodded my head and said:

—*Yes, sir.*

He told me further that I work as a manager in a supermarket, but I would retire within three days. Again, I ran into hard temptation and again he told me:

—*Don't look at me so peculiarly, you will sign a contract of retirement within three days and on the fourth day you will come back to me to inform me of this. This is in your destiny, whether you want this or not, you will have to accept it.*

He said further:

—*Your foster daughter, whom you call your own daughter, is going on a far journey; she is the mother of one child. That journey should lead somehow to Paris.*

At the time this was completely impossible, since my daughter and son-in-law were working and again he explained to me mildly:

—*This is the state of affairs, Stojanka, there is much political uncertainty, your son-in-law and your daughter will be laid off and they will look for residence in France; that is Paris.*

I asked when and he replied:

—*Quickly, by August they will already be there. And here, in less than a month and a half, one will be jobless and then the other. You will have some family relations, who will switch them to this path. Don't stand in their way, let them go, such is their destiny.*

Furthermore, he told me that my husband is a former official and is now retired. He said I will have a little trouble concerning a question with my housing, and that my husband consumes much alcohol, which brings us into big quarrels at home.

He told me that my son was unemployed, but not to worry, in late fall, early winter, around the New Year, he sees a path for him and employment. He told me that seven spells have been cast upon me, and that I am not at all aware of how naive I am, but in a short while all would be made known to me, and that I will be able to see and tell my friends from my foes. And, he also saw the death of a person very close to me.

But, I should not worry at all, that this person is much older, and it is possibly my mother, since I do not have a grandmother. Also, that this person is on a journey and will not make it through the winter.

Since then, all that he said has literally come true. I am retired, which may be checked. My foster daughter is in Paris, exactly as Mr. Ivica said. My mother is dying, she has not died yet, but the day of her passing is quickly approaching. Actually, everything that he said has all come true.

Today, I am full of a love for life. I have come to know myself, I feel as if after all of this, had I not turned to our Mr. Ivica, all would have been much more tragic, but here you see, thank God everything ended well.

I admit that I have become a great believer, I believe in God, and the power that I am sure only God, and no one else, gives to our Sir. Once again, many thanks to our Mr. Ivica.

Mira Sekulić

In December 1991, I read an article in *Vikend* that a prophet had appeared, named Ivica Prokić.

I should mention that I also work in an alternative field, I do coffee cup readings and I think I have psychic abilities.

When I went, I have to admit it was provocatively, to see what kind of a person he was. Was he a charlatan or did he truly possess the abilities the newspaper wrote about? I came to him, I must say, on a Friday.

That day when I left, I told the people who were coming to me that I would be absent, in order to have my own fortune told. And so without a notice, I went to see Mr. Ivica Prokić.

To my great surprise, when I walked in to see him and sat on that chair, he first looked at the flame of a burning candle, then looked at me straight in the eyes, before returning his gaze to the mirror and said:

> —*You bitch, why do you do this?! This is not your God given gift, why do you cheat people? At the same time you came to cheat me also! How much does a treatment cost now, one coffee cup reading?*

I must admit I started shaking that instant, I immediately realized that I was facing no ordinary man. He started insulting me and said:

> —*I'm going to throw you out!*

This is why I now advise all those, who think they could prevent him from doing what he does, that they are very small in comparison. He cannot be lied to and he does truly see everything.

Bear in mind, those insults I heard, had I been anywhere else, I might have gotten into a fight over it, but I listened to all of this and despised myself.

I was bound by some kind of an invisible force, and I could not say anything nor tell my reason for coming, because he saw it all, and drove it away with his insulting words. I kept on sitting as if welded onto that chair. I thought that even if I gave him all the wealth in the world, I could never keep doing the work I had been doing until then. I no longer do it.

With Ivica, I came to know myself. He later explained that everyone can see some figures in the grounds of the coffee, but that this should not be charged for. Later, he set me free and cheered me up saying; if I had company over and did it for fun, and if I got some of it right, people could leave a small amount behind for coffee or cigarettes.

He further said:

> —I would only trust in the ability of one man to see in the grounds of a coffee cup. He is actually in this very city. It is old grandpa, Vale. My dear Mira, he does not look at the coffee grounds, it is a tool for him to orient himself and then he speaks.

But these are not his words, his spirit guide tells him what is going on with the person that he is predicting for at the time.

He does not charge for his work, this has been given to him and

166

he does it because it has been given to him as a gift. Try doing as he does, and you will see that your own Angel will speak from your mouth, and then results will come that people will accept one day.

As long as you hope to get rich by this as a business and live at other people's expense, and cheat them as you've done so far, you will be whipped where it hurts the most.

You can see it for yourself; you have two children and have big problems with those kids. Police are after your sons. You see yourself that everything is taken away and does not last forever. If you listen to me, you will do what you do without charging.

I see in these difficult times that you charge 2,000 Dinaris. Is this really what you need when you will spend it all on hospitals, lawyers and in the courts? Your husband left you. Had you been able to predict your own misfortune, you would see the kind of nightmare you have been in.

You see, Mira, you drive a car, you have BMW, I do not even have a bicycle and like all the ordinary people, I ride the tram and bus. What's more, I do not even use a taxi, unless I really need it.

Well, now take a look at who is more powerful; is it I, or you who have materialized all this. You see, you have everything, but you do not have the blessing.

I must confess I was shivering after all those words. Since then, I have been regularly visiting our Sir, admiring his work, as I have said publicly.

There are no longer any treatments, and in my home great grace has come. My son did many idiotic things up to June of this year. Just as Ivica said, my son came home and said:

—*Mom, I'll work as a waiter on a ship.*

And this is where my son can be found today. The other one no longer takes drugs, I have regained my peace, for which I can only thank our Sir and the Lord God. Thank you!

Ankica Tot

My story is this: I should tell you that I am a refugee from Vukovar. I came to Sir after reading all about him in *Arena*. I took along a photo of my late son and came to see what Mr. Ivica would tell me. When I walked inside, I took a seat on a chair and gave him the photo.

He looked into the flame of the candle and said:

—*What do you want to know about this man?*

And I asked him to tell me where he is. He looked at me angrily, opened the door, which he never does as people later told me, and said:

—*People, you see this woman, she brought me a picture of her son who was buried several months ago and now lays in a grave. Decide what we should do with her. Can you see the evil that has entered into her so that she cannot even let a dead man have his peace in the grave?*

I almost fainted. Such pain crept into my heart, what right did I have to disturb the child that I had buried, and especially a man whom I had never known until then. People were abhorred, and one of them asked:

—Woman, why are you doing this?

I said I did not know. Later he told me:

—You have completed your mission, you may go, but never do this again.

After coming there, I pondered over this for so long. Finally I gathered the courage to return to Mr. Ivica, to give him my deepest gratitude and to apologize for the injustice on my part.

Sandra Kos

I came to the Sir at Tuškanova Street in April 1992, since *Vikend* wrote about him. I brought along a picture of my husband who had gone missing. It was very crowded inside, so I brooded and waited to be called. I must say I came there at 7 o'clock in the morning and was received at half past one in the afternoon.

Whenever he would walk out, I would hide so he would not see me. I could tell in the waiting room already, talking to people, that others had come to this great man who sees and knows everything, and I was tormented as I realized the truth. I was afraid of him saying to me that my husband had been killed, although up to that point there was no official announcement.

I came to hear the truth, but I must confess that I was afraid of that truth. I have one child. We were married for five years, in a happy marriage, and we were very much in love. I was so afraid of walking in to see Sir, but waited until the time came, and at half past one I came in to him, among the last.

He walked out and the first thing he said was:

—*Sandra, you have been hiding enough, now you must enter!*

You could imagine what I felt. I entered, stiff with excitement, and he said to me:

—*Give me your husband's photo and his details.*

Then he began speaking further. I remembered every word, as follows:

—*Your husband went missing at the time of the fall of Vukovar.*

I asked him only if he was alive, and he replied:

—*I can't see.*

He went on saying:

—*My Sandra, he was in a hospital in Vukovar, wounded. I see him coming to a barrack. He is separated here and disappears without a trace. He is in a fog, which I cannot penetrate. I also see a house, there is a fence around that house, and there are guards in that house. Not even I can enter here spiritually. Wait for better days. I cannot claim that your husband is either dead or alive. I'll check in the documents. You are looking for him ardently, you have covered it all, but I do not see him on any records. He is not listed for shifts, he is not among the living, neither among the dead, and I only come across him listed amongst the missing. That is, officially, you have not been notified of him being killed.*

I cannot tell you anything more, but go home and keep your son safe. You are not from Zagreb. I see you live near some large body of water; it could be the sea. You live there in someone else's house; it is like a country cottage.

It all happened precisely as he said, verbatim. Now it was only left to say whether he was alive or dead. After a month, I came again and begged him to see what he could, and he told me:

—You found out from someone that these people were transferred to the Aleksinac mines.

It was true, word for word. I found this out and it was also immediately confirmed. Actually, I was surprised and then realized that this gentleman knew nothing about me, and such information was not known, but here he was telling me all about it.

Again, he took my husband's photograph and said:

—Sandra, he is somewhere under the ground. A living heart is beating, but what does this mean? Maybe he is hiding in some shaft, or working in some mine. I do not see him as being free, but it symbolizes that he is alive at this time.

He only said:

—Well, there will be luck in 1993.

It now remains to be seen what will actually happen in 1993. I am waiting, but I really have not received any information other than from Ivica, who to this day does not say whether he is alive or dead. He always refuses, saying:

—*I do not see this, the situation is not resolved yet. When the case is settled, you will know when the time comes.*

This is why I stringently wish to write about what I have experienced in my search for my missing husband. I believe my husband is alive, and if only Ivica could confirm this, I would believe it even more. But for now, he holds silent and says, when the time for it comes, you will know everything. Many thanks to our Mr. Ivica.

Milica Pavlović

Quite by accident I came to a shop in Utrine in order to buy some fruit and inside a saleswoman served me very kindly. The saleswoman's name was Danica, and although we did not known each other, she said to me:

—*You are our regular customer; tell me, do you work in the social pension insurance?*

I replied saying I was a lawyer there and she asked me to help her with something relating to her mother's case. I said yes, we have her documents with us today. So we spoke about it a bit.

She asked:

—*Misses, when will these documents reach my mother?*

I said it would be in three days and that they are favorably resolved. I smiled, accompanying the saleswoman as she began to carefully choose the fruit and she said to me:

—Today it is on me, and I am taking some fruit directly to Ivica at 28 Tuškanova Street.

This probably meant nothing, but I suspected that it was someone who had taken a bribe for the case that I was legally resolving, but apparently I was wrong. I asked Danica, who is this man? She continued the story of how her mother learned about Mr. Ivica at 28 Tuškanova Street, and how she went to him. She said everything she was told coincided exactly with everything that happened.

I became interested in this man, and listened to the story carefully. Afterwards, I took his address and told my friends the story. They supported me and nine of us went to see Mr. Ivica. There were a lot of people there, but not as many as there are today.

I should mention that this happened on June 15, 1990. From all of us, Ivica first took in my sister. She then worked for the Yugoslav army. He told her that she was married and a mother of two kids. Also, that she would lose her job one day and go on the road.

Then, a more detailed story followed; I told everyone, some believed at the time, and some did not. He took me last and said that I was the greatest believer and that only I was to be worked with, because all of the others would laugh at him.

He predicted it all. He admitted every one of us. Notably, one from our group was there for her child's sake, and he told her:

—Madam, no one can help your child. This one is 18 years old, but acts like a child of one year.

Essentially, in a tally, the information about the past was first rate, he spoke of the present as it really was, but no one believed him about the future. Bear in mind, out of the nine of us, there were Muslims, Serbs, as well as Croats.

He told everyone what they personally had coming, but for future events, trust me, even I was in doubt and didn't know whether to believe him or not.

After a year, everything started coming true. Just as the sirens went off, we were at Ivica's. Then, we were convinced that this is not some sort of charlatanism, but in truth this man actually sees and helps.

What's more, in that year 1990, he said to me:

—Milica, you are not married and will never get married. You have it all, you can do everything, but you can never have children and a family. You cannot because this has not been given to you.

He told me:

—You have had a miscarriage three times. You have had several relationships that lasted for a while, but they always ended tragically.

I then asked how this was done to me, and he said:

—You see, a white wedding dress has been buried for you in an

unknown grave. This has been done with expertise. Since you already had surgery, this means children have already been taken away from you, and you will not get married. In your best years, you will retire.

When you least expect it, then you will leave. You have already done something with regards to your pension, and you will finish it but not now, in about two years. Finally, you will retire and will no longer live in this city. Something will happen so you will have to leave the city.

This all happened, and everything occurred just as our Mister said it would. I actually felt that I would be in a different city and now I live there. Many thanks to Mr. Ivica, and to whomever does not believe, may you not have to come, go through and pass by all that we had to go through first. Thank you!

Drago Damjanić

My coming to Mr. Ivica was very specific. I am from Dubrovnik. It was Sunday and I met an old acquaintance from college. He asked me to a cafe for a drink, carrying a book in his hand. We sat down and I asked him about the book, and he replied that he had just returned from Zagreb. He went there to see some man, and he told me all about it at the cafe.

Then he told me.

—You see, this man, Ivica, published a book. I can tell you, I was in a hotel for three days until I was admitted. There were masses; I never believed that there were people who could prophesize and foresee the future.

I asked my friend what it said in the book, and he answered that he read it while waiting for a plane from Zagreb to Dubrovnik. He said that it was really well written, and it would not be a bad idea for me to read it. I took the book and brought it home. In the evening, I started reading it and fell asleep, not managing to finish it.

The event I am about to describe happened right in Dubrovnik, at my apartment. In the morning I got up and as I turned on the faucet, it fell apart and a rush of water began to spray in the bathroom. I was scared, and then suddenly I saw the man from the photo on the book I was reading. He came right over to me, like he was just there close by. He put his hand on the faucet and the water stopped. I had my problem solved that instant.

He just said:

> —*I will see you tomorrow at my place in Zagreb. Come sonny, you need my help.*

I was completely stupefied. I took the book and immediately began reading.

In the meantime, I booked a flight at the Dubrovnik airport. Then, I immediately looked through all the telephone directories for the phone number of the Mister. Without success, I ended up sending him a telegram, informing him that I would be there at half past twelve. I asked him to wait for me, and not to leave, since I was coming especially to see him from Dubrovnik.

You can imagine what I felt when I arrived at the airport at 12:05 p.m. I paid for a taxi in order to get there by half past twelve, just as I had notified the Mister. I walked in. A man opened the door, greeted me and I did not know with whom I was speaking. I thought he was a gentleman who must work here. And, as I began to explain my situation to him, he could not hear me out because the doorbell rang and the telegram arrived. Then, that same man went into the other room, and announced:

—*Sir, a telegram came for you.*

When the other man walked out of that room into the waiting room, where I was with the other people, I can tell you that I bristled. He was the same man who repaired my faucet that morning in Dubrovnik.

Taking the telegram in his hands, he looked at me and said:

—*The man has arrived before the telegram arrives.*

Please know that the person to whom I spoke earlier could not have said anything to the Mister about my case, but he obviously already knew I was in his waiting room.

He just said:

—*Boy, I will admit you.*

He did not even look at me.

—*It is your telegram that has just arrived, but you arrived before it.*

I was very surprised. When I walked in, he received me and in a calm tone spoke all the words that needed to be said.

I was shocked when he told me:

—So, you need to travel to New York in two days.

Hereby, I want to say that this gentleman has a power that materializes everywhere it is needed. Indeed, no one can lie about anything to him. Many thanks for what he has done for me, and this is why I bring up my case, because it should be recorded in history.

Darko & Kata Bošnjak

The story of Darko:

I heard about Ivica from my godmother a year and a half ago, and came to him while he was still at Tuškanova Street. When I came, it was by myself, and after a while he took me into his room and told me; trust me, your name is ... Darko.

—How old are you, sonny? He asked me.

—Fifty-eight. I answered.

Then he continued:

—All is not well in your house. Your house is under a great curse. You have a son who is in a hospital; you have all declared him insane. But this boy is not crazy; he even went to university. A woman that saw him coming from town with a girl cast this on him. She thought to marry her daughter to him, and threw a great curse on your house. Your wife is ill, you are ill, your daughter is married, and you do not have happiness in

your marriage.

He told me about my entire family. The cow would give birth, and the calf would die. There was a burglary in our house, and he spoke of all of the ways that I had suffered. Then he stopped and said to me:

—*A golf car that was stolen from you last year, in three days, the police will inform you that the car has been found in Rijeka. You will receive the car back. You, Darko, have worked in Germany for over 30 years. I see myself in your house, and I will come as your guest when you get your first pension.*

My dear friends, in three days, I got back the golf car just as Ivica had said. My son got out of the hospital and is no longer on any pills. He married a girl, and he is employed at the Ministry of Internal Affairs as a lawyer. It is not peaceful in my house, but it has such grace that I invited Ivica, and he paid me a visit on August 10, 1993, exactly when I received my first pension. He was my dearest guest.

I asked him:

—*Sir, what don't you have that I could give you?*

Please, he only took some corncobs to cook at home and nothing else. And even though he was about 150 kilometers away from Zagreb, he would not even take anything for fuel. This visit meant a lot to me. Now, in November, when we are expecting a newcomer in our house, as my daughter-in-law will give birth, I have invited Mr. Ivica, who will be my most cherished guest, should he agree to attend. When I invited him, he just smiled and said:

—We will see.

There is no longer any curse on my house. In the town where I live, I know about twenty fellow residents telling the same story as I do, and indeed this man cannot be repaid for all that he is doing for us.

The story of Kata:

I have seen and strongly believe my Darko. With a woman's curiosity, I went to Ivica after a month and a half, but only after my husband left for Germany. He was working in Munich then.

When I arrived, the first thing he asked me:

—Well, Kata, for God's sake, even you come to me. What have you brought me?

Dear God, I said to myself, this man has never seen me and he already knows I'm bringing him something, and that my dearest has already been to see him. On my way there, I had thought to myself that I would not say anything to him, but he struck me down just as I was entering. I saw that one cannot lie, and so I said:

—Well there, Sir, I've come to thank you. The golf car has been returned to us.

To this he replied:

—You didn't come for this; you thought your husband was lying, so you came to see for yourself.

And then, I gave him what I brought from my house. He received it with a smile and said:

> —*Good, Kata, thank you, but in a few days your son is coming out, he is a very good boy. Give him this water to drink, and sew this into his bed and you will see what happens.*

Since then, we are constantly visiting Ivica and now, he has even been to our home. Our neighbors found out that he came to see us, which was difficult for them because we did not take him over to see them. This does not mean Ivica will not come again, and visit those people who really wish for it.

Many thanks to our Ivica. If God had given us more people like Ivica, no one would ever be as heartbroken as we were.

Višnja Majdić

We have been coming for about a year and a half, both my mother and I, and we are doing well, so well that I've personally been to Sir's house. I would like to talk about what went on in our lives back then at the time. This much I exclusively wish to say; my father had a stroke in June of this year. With his left side paralyzed, he was carried over to the hospital and ended up completely immobilized.

I came to Ivica immediately the next day. He looked at me and said:

> —*Višnja, I cannot bring back a dead man. He has all but been taken away.*

Trust me, he could not have known what had happened and he did not even know why I came that morning. But, he told me everything, just as if he had personally been there, himself.

> —*Your father is immobile. This I cannot do, only God can restore him. I can see that he is already in the hospital and I see he is in the hands of doctors.*

What else could I do but beg. The only genuine words of consolation were:

> —*Dear child, go; should you feel that there is an improvement in three days then we will succeed.*

I can freely say that Ivica was here in our apartment, as I have shown to all the witnesses. My father walks now and has personally had coffee with Ivica.

Truly amazing! We are very grateful.

Ademi Ismaili

My nationality is Albanian, and my family and I live and work in Varaždin. I read about Ivica Prokić in 1992, in *Arena*, and so I immediately came. Ivica admitted me and instantly identified my medical history. My back was so painful that it almost led me to insanity. There were fights and clashes in the family.

With my very arrival to Ivica at Tuškanova Street, I realized that this was not an ordinary man, but a man who really helps and knew what was going on with my family then. I came several times; I came without prior notice and I always waited. Ivica would take me by the hands or give me a liter of water, and I did precisely as I was told.

Today, after a year, my family is so happy that we always go to visit him. We own a pastry shop and whenever I come, it is our honor to bring cakes. I have never seen him happier than when I hand over the pastries. He has truly helped us a lot and we shall always come here.

Many thanks to Mr. Ivica.

Marta Zelić

I am Marta Zelić, I came to Srebrnjak 1 purely by chance on June 4, 1994, when I found out from my sister and some others. I would never wish for anyone in this world to go through the turmoil I have experienced. For three years, I was suffering and going to all kinds of hospitals. I have been married for 12 years, and in the beginning I had my one and only child, my son, Boris. Since then, and until I came to Mr. Prokić, I did not have any other children. Why, I do not know.

There was no cure for my illness. From severe bone pains, to pain in my backbone, I was in pain throughout my whole body. What this was like for me, may God never give, not even to my enemy. I have seen all the Swiss doctors. Every doctor had given up on me and they would change their diagnosis each time I came. It could not have been any worse.

When I saw our prophet, the situation started to shift substantially.

You know, my dear ones, I would not mind walking from Lucerne, Switzerland to see Mr. Prokic, and not only me, but everyone I have sent and continue sending. Not only has he spoken words of praise to me, he has also blessed me for being a great messenger. But, then at the time, I truly did not understand what Mr. Prokić was talking about.

My God, it is as if I was asleep, but it has all become very clear to me now. I am currently in his family home, and these good hosts have welcomed me like I was their sister. I cannot describe this beauty and wonder.

What is my life today; I am a happy wife, as well as a soon to be mother of my second child due in February 1995. And, what else can I say, when you can see how I have eagerly rushed over as if I were 15 years old, just to say something for documentation in this book.

Out of all these people, it is my great privilege to receive the first honor to tell you about all of this. I love our Ivica so very much, not only I, but also all who know him, especially my son, Boris, and my husband, Pero. We call him brother, and God forbid that anyone says anything against our prophet; I would poke his eyes out. We have faith in him and we had no faith when all this happened.

Just like that, he never charged me a single penny; that is not a single franc. Mr. Prokić looks at all of us as if we are his family. I thank Mr. Prokić, and those dearest to him, and our people, for we all love him just as he loves us all. Would we be here today if we did not believe in him?

He guides us into a brighter future, and he gave me a new life. My new life, my yet unborn child, is of the heart and showing below my heart. This is the seal on all of this. I send out great regards to all of you, as well as to Mr. Prokić, personally. People from Switzerland love him immensely and believe in him.

Pero Blažan

I am Pero Blažan. Please, I have faith in Mr. Prokic, not just me, but also my sisters Bernarda, Serafinka, Angela and Manda, who are in Switzerland. Not only do we have faith in him, we simply love him. We have been coming to him since March 13, 1993. It has been almost two years since I, my sisters and all those who joined us, have been coming to our Mr. Prokić.

Does he help us?

Would we be coming for so long if we did not believe this to be so? Our problems were various. I would not like to get into details right now, out of the very respect for our great and renowned Ivica Prokić. But, I do say I trust in him and believe in him. You, yourself, know that we would not have come just like that, nor would we have remained so long. We simply adore, believe in and love him.

The future that is coming is before us. We shall never leave him, but shall trustworthily enter the key, the golden key, the golden time, along with our Mr. Prokić.

Zora Radić

I am not from this city. I went once to Ivica, spoke with him, and when I went home I was indeed commenting on it to my friends. I was just enthralled by what he told me.

My coming to see him was regarding my husband's infidelity. He told me everything in Zagreb, word for word, about how my husband had left me and gone to a different town where he has been living with his mistress. Even though he had two children with me, his mistress gave birth to a child by him, and my children were always complaining and wishing to see their father. That is why I came to Ivica to hear what he would say.

All told, he said my husband had left me, he was not in my town, but he would come back to me in three days, begging to make amends. What was not clear to me was how this man could come back to me when he had a child with his mistress. I should explain that we were divorced. When I came home to my town, I could not tell my children where I had been. I just sat down and watched television, and suddenly, Ivica appeared in my room and said:

—Zora, your husband will come to you in the morning.

Bear in mind that I was watching television. Ivica came and appeared in that room. Just as he arrived, he vanished. The following morning, I intentionally did not want to go to work. I stayed at home to see whether this was all a figment of my imagination or whether my husband would actually come. Believe me, he appeared at 8 o'clock in the morning on the doorstep, and said he had come because he wanted me to take him back.

This is reality and truth. I told him that his place was with his

186

children and that he could stay. Within three days, we got a message that the child who had been born was dying. He was very nervous and said:

—What more does she want from me, if it is that child's destiny to die, let him die, we shall bury him.

And, so he did not go. He thought it was some trick by her. He kept saying how his heart had been tied, and he told me:

—Zora, it was as if I was spellbound. Did I really not come back home for a year and a half? Does she think I will be so foolish again, like when she has an itch I will run right back?

And he did not go.

At around 4 o'clock in the afternoon, we received a telegram that the child had died. Even then he did not go. We got remarried and now live happily. We can only thank Mr. Ivica. Not that I'm only his believer, but so much more than that. I am willing to give my right hand for Mr. Ivica. This man is so worthy. I can understand everything, but I cannot understand how I was able to see him in my house, and how it all played out just as he said it would. Therefore, it has materialized, and when I was truly desperate. My family and I, once again, thank Mr. Ivica very much.

Damjan Mitrović

I constantly work with these people and hear all their stories. People who are coming to Mr. Ivica, either once or several times, are so happy and delighted. People returning always tell new people waiting for the first time that one cannot lie to Mr. Ivica. He anticipates all visits and knows why a person comes. I am not saying that Mr. Ivica is always in a good mood; that is he is always smiling. He can be enraged sometimes, and I have witnessed that he is most disturbed by lies.

Lies such as, when a wife or a husband wants Ivica to say that their spouse has a lover or a mistress. I was present on several occasions when a woman brought her husband into the room to see Ivica. All is well until you hear his voice in a raised tone. Then, I know what will follow; next he is warning this wife that her husband would not do it for anything in the world. He affirms that the man is honest, that he does not have a mistress and declares that she is ill, in need of a psychiatrist, and not him. Then, he is very abrupt and immediately throws her out. This lasts for about a minute or two, and then the people who have come and witness this for the first time are very frightened.

Right away, I would calm these people down, as well as those who have already been to the Sir. I explain, saying that he is not like this normally, but this person offended him by wanting him to lie, so he rejected it and drove her out.

Another that he anticipates and sees is a sneaker, by that, I mean a reporter. He does not notify anyone beforehand, he just comes out and instantly warns that there is a snoop among them. He says that he does not wish to give any advertisement about himself, and does not want to talk to the press.

Why he does not like them, I do not know. It is the same matter when someone comes provocatively. In that very instant he opens the door and says that uninvited and unwanted guests have no place here. It is better for them to go away by themselves rather than having him throw them out. Trust me, I have always seen, just as the door closes, one or two people leaving. And I observed it the wiser, always hearing one of them say to the other:

—Let's go, he's dangerous! It's better not to get in his way, if he does not mess with us, why should we care. It's better not to come into conflict with such a person.

Believe me, in this last half a year, as long as I've been working for Ivica, I've seen at least 20 such cases. He does not allow politics inside either; he immediately drives such people out. Those waiting think that because he is in a different room, he will not come out and attack. Here you go, this is why it remains so very peaceful in that little waiting room of his.

Joško Prlić

I should immediately say that I work in Germany. I've been there for 26 years. I am married, a father of two, and I became ill eight years ago. When I read about Ivica Prokić in *Arena*, I called the editorial office and asked for Mr. Ivica's phone number. They told me that Ivica works at 28 Tuškanova Street, from 8:00 a.m. to 3:00 p.m, and that it was not possible to make an appointment by phone. I just went there as a bluff. To my great surprise, as I had not expected it, there were many people waiting. I tried getting ahead in the line as a foreigner, but this did not work. I saw that people came from everywhere, and so I somehow managed to ask for help from a man who works for him and I was admitted.

My medical diagnosis was very negative. I had stomach pains, pressure in my chest, and nervousness; and then he gave me his diagnosis. He said that my navel had a foul smell, that it was an unprotected chakra, that I had severe strangulation in my chest, and that I had headaches, which he identified as did the medical reports.

He smiled and said:

—*You're not from around here. You live abroad.*

No one could have told him this beforehand. I told him I live in Germany. He stated exactly how long I had been living there, that I have children, a wife, and that there was a big disagreement in my house. That it all started 8–10 years ago. Everything was correct.

I should mention that he gave me a bundle of some kind to carry with me, and a bottle of water. He took my hands, and I must admit that an intense current flowed from his hands, and I cannot even describe today what actually was happening. This same effect was even felt throughout my house in Germany, for my family felt a relaxation. Since then, I have visited Ivica three more times. I always come from Germany and always get admitted. Now, I feel very, very well. My pains have disappeared and after the New Year, I started to work. I had not been working for exactly five years. I have always been on sick leave, but on January 15, 1993, I started working again.

I wanted to express all this and publicly thank Mr. Ivica. We are all grateful to him, my wife, and my children. Many thanks for returning the peace in our house.

We no longer fight; now, we have become a fine and harmonious family. I must emphasize again that if I had not believed so much, my healing would probably not have occurred. Once again, I thank all those who have written about him. This is how I came to know about a man, this man, who genuinely helped me. Once again, thank you very much, Mr. Ivica.

Vlado Polek

In August, I read an article in the magazine, *Erotika*. This article about Mr. Ivica told about how he helps all kinds of people. I went to see him, but should mention by that time I had looked for help everywhere and sought help from everyone. I went to Bosnia and saw a variety of healers, imams, fortunetellers, and those doing bioenergetics, but when I came here I was very surprised.

After I walked into Mr. Ivica's workroom, he immediately told me everything that was happening, what I was suffering from, and not only me, but also all of my family.

He told me that I have two households, one outside Zagreb in one town, and one in Zagreb where we all live. We are normally in Zagreb, and in the other town we have a weekend cottage. He described that cottage, just as he did the house in Zagreb. He said I was employed and that I am a special man. And, I suffer from a backache every single day. And, this was all true.

Then he told me:

—*My brother, you have seven chakras on you.*

And I asked him if he would help me. He said:

—*That is what you decide, not me.*

191

I noticed when I came home, the biggest surprise was my father, who said to me:

—*Vlado, you must have gone somewhere.*

At the time, it was like something happened to me, and I thought I would prefer to fly than to walk because of all the beauty I felt. Then, I told him about the complete event, and my father said:

—*Son, take me to this man.*

I took him, but was a little provocative about it. When the old man went in, imagine, he was told the same as I was, and Ivica did not even know he was my father. We have truly been convinced. Since August 1992, which I give testimony to today, that man has helped all of us a great deal.

Those discomforts are gone, and I act like the most normal person. I wish to say publicly that whenever I have come to Ivica, my father would not know of my visit, but would always feel it. Whenever I return back home, he asks:

—*Have you been to see Ivica today?*

I always smile and say:

—*How do you know?*

And, dad replies:

—*Telepathy, my son! You just keep going to that man, he helps us immensely.*

And I will go for as long as I have a need. Many thanks to Ivica, and to the people from *Erotika*, thank you very much. I would finish by safely saying that if we had not believed, my family and I, we would not have what we have today.

Nikola Iliać

When I read in *Vikend* that there was a man in Zagreb named Ivica, I immediately went to see him. I must say I am a man from a rural family. My problems were numerous. I suffered from severe insomnia. My chest felt like it was laden with cement. In the house, there was such nervousness, fights every day, and it was actually hell. As for my assets, all were in a deadlock. I worked at a sawmill. It was my own sawmill, which did not work out at the time. I lost everything I had.

When I came to Mr. Ivica, he received me very kindly and said everything exactly as it was.

He told me:

> —*Nikola, when you come next time, and you will be coming to see me several times; bring me several kilograms of grit, and a bit of salt and I will make a mixture for you to add to your assets and everything will rejuvenate.*

And that is what I did. Trust me, it has been almost a year since I've known Mr. Ivica, and great prosperity has come to my home. All the troubles have ceased. I keep coming, whenever I feel the need, and am very grateful for all that he has done for me. I give my many thanks to everyone who has written, and especially to the man who has helped me.

And finally . . .

Since I have already explained to my patients how it is that I help, how I do it all and manage to materialize so that they see me appearing close at hand, even though I am many, many kilometers away from them, I would jokingly add this:

> —*Well, if I do not materialize what I do and I do not take money, what else can I do but materialize myself where I ought to be.*

CHAPTER 6

FROM THE OTHER SIDE
OF THE WALL

THE SECRETS OF THE
UNDERGROUND WORLD

It has always been that people are afraid of what both day and night have to offer. I have already described that there are positive and negative energies. Negative energy is also referred to as black magic and the people from the underground world are just this, while we call the positive that which God has given.

Now, we need to find out how someone can be closed in by evil, so that there is no escape. This is what I will describe here.

This happens at a location between Niš and Prokuplje.

Here, there is a wall, invisible to man. At this site, evil brings people from all over the world, to turn them into numerous varieties of animals. This looks like something from long ago, when there were people who ruled villages, with their own servants and many treasures of wealth.

These people, the souls of these people, are enslaved, just as it used to be in the past when slavery ruled. For such people, when they are incarcerated in this prison, they expiate by suffering; they can be heavily whipped or killed. In their physical body; as they are whipped, beaten, consumed, and abused, they become psychologically ill. And, as the guards torture them, they become physically very unstable, and though they seek help everywhere, that help is always unsuccessful. They withdraw into themselves, becoming hateful, speaking ill, thinking ill, and manipulate the emotional life of the unfortunate. They are unsociable, and are miserable in their own emotional life. They remain unmarried, all is closed for them, and no one can get away and heal.

The only salvation is great love.

Why did I say that this location is between Niš and Prokuplje?

It is because I have been to the other side of this wall and seen it. I was told that there is such a climate here that the negative energy chose this as the most suitable location for its prison. People from all over the world come to serve their punishment here. There is no other location, only the one on this site.

I have spoken that the entrance to the underground world is between Karlovac and Zagreb. Between Kruševac and Niš, one of the Cross-Mountains stands and this is where the new civilization will begin.

The Kosovo field is an infernal cauldron. I guarantee it, as I saw that the entire Kosovo field has oil swimming underneath it, because there is negative energy. The same goes for Kuwait. Wherever there is an oil deposit, this is key that something is boiling there; something is going on in the bowels of Earth, who has to endure it all.

The souls of the deceased boil here.

I have already mentioned where the prisons are, where people are thrown into boiling oil, and we call this hell, where the new civilization begins, and where one enters the underground world. Now, I must tell and explain what this ugly and detestable parasite can do, how strong it is, and what hate it can create in man.

If a person would just look around himself a little bit, and see that nothing comes out of hatred, he would not be doing what the negative energy dictates for him to do.

Whosoever comes into the underground world is bound for judgment. All those who have stolen, cheated, lied, all those who have sinned for personal gain, all those who have been subject to vices and transgressions against the human race, all enter the underground world. Anyone who commits such deeds in this physical existence already partly enters the underworld, and their Spirit guide is imprisoned, so that the forces of Evil can operate more successfully. Anyone who seeks only material goods is also descending on the path to the underworld.

There are those, however, who do not complete the tasks they've received in the underground world. When they reincarnate, they turn overnight to a life of drinking, drugs, promiscuity, and then they approach crime and get blood on their hands.

Above us is a spiritual world, alike to our own, but not materialized. Good people can see it.

It is the world that belongs to those who are good. They continue their existence in it after this physical human life. This spiritual world is very close to us in the physically existing one. Actually, the boundary between the visible, our physical world, and the unseen spiritual world is very small and thin. I would compare it to a window's glass. On this side is the physical, and on the other side is the spiritual.

Many things and events lead an individual into the curse of damnation and karmic punishment. One of them is marital infidelity, since spouses are given to each other karmically. The question is, why does infidelity even occur?

I must say, adultery done by the woman is more often the case, regardless of whether the adultery results in breaking up the marriage, or whether the spouses resume living their lives together. Adultery occurs with those women who have had a male harem in their past lives. In their current physical incarnation, they have two men, a husband and a lover.

Actually, adulteresses in this incarnation take revenge on male lovers for what they have done in previous lives, although they are not conscious of it. It is not rare for the lover to even be close with the deceived husband, as the woman draws life energy from both, slowly but surely destroying them.

In unfaithful marriages, female children are not born, only male offspring and usually only one, or two at most. Adulteresses usually have thin ankles, they are never large, and their appearance is not much different from other women. Their lover is usually thin, malnourished, and very lively and carefree sexually.

As for the husband, he refuses to see his wife's infidelity, because he is focused on creating material wealth, and in his sexual life, he is prone to relations with minors. The cheated on husband is given all the success and achievement of his desires as compensation for his wife's adultery.

In such a triangle, the lover usually deteriorates, withering with exhaustion and actually goes through the worst, falling ill and unable to die. He gives all he has to his lover, neglecting his own family, if he has one.

The punishment of an adulteress comes in her lifetime, usually around the age of 55. Severe changes occur within her. With her son's marriage, Evil enters her house, she falls ill, and all that she has acquired during her life is lost. She physically deteriorates, as others take away all that she gained from her second relationship. She must suffer for what she has done, and her lineage comes to a tragic end and is not preserved.

Regarding the lover's offspring, his own wife usually despises him, giving her whole being's attention to the first direct descendants, and then to her grandsons and granddaughters. Here, carried within the offspring, there is usually the seed to become an eminent and famous intellectual.

The son of the lover is just, sincere, and has an honest wife. Good children are born in their marriage, and the female offspring marry well.

The lover can only be blinded by the adulteress for a maximum of 23 physical human years, and once it all passes, his children forgive him for everything that he has done, knowing that he was misled and weak.

Every household needs to have its head. Should this person lead the household, as he should, this is how the vine of lineage successfully blooms after him. Throughout his further incarnations, he can make up to three faults. If he makes more than three faults, then in the next incarnation there will not be any descendants, and this is how one household within one vine ends and the householder's soul goes into darkness.

Reincarnation can only be restored to the mortal world after many centuries of travel in the dark, because the punishment is meant to smarten them up. That is why it is said that each household can only bring ruin upon itself.

THE ANIMAL WORLD

I saw myself floating above a flock of sheep, spanning out on all sides. Among them were the sheepdogs that guarded them. And, with them were shepherds with donkeys.

There were also some strange people here, wrapped in close-fitting garb.

The voice asked me:

—*Can you count them all?*

—*No.* I admitted.

The voice continued:

—*They are the sheep that you must guard from the wolves. Tell me, which animal slaughters more than it needs to eat? Which kills, but does not have to?*

—I do not know.

—The wolf. It is ruled by negative energy.

Then the voice went on:

—But beware; man also kills without having the right to do so! People can also be wolves.

It further told me:

—The cat is also governed by negative energy.

I was surprised:

—Then, why does man let the cat into the house?

—God has ordained cats to kill mice and rats.

Our animals see more than the people do, they see almost as much as those invisible guards who see the ghosts, which sneak up on people to harm them. So, some animal companions also see them.

Dogs will never bark at positive vibrations, but they will froth from barking and anger when they see apparitions, invisible to human eyes. Dogs are in this world in order to guard and warn, although most people disregard these warnings. That is why dogs often bark with all their strength, and the person gets upset because in his blindness it seems as if the dog is only barking at the wind.

As for the cats, they are negative energy. And dogs are the opposite.

Snakes are not as a man sees them with his physical eyes. No matter how small they might be, they are always much bigger in the spiritual world. Their true size can be seen by clairvoyants, and by horses as well. For instance, a snake a few centimeters in length using physical sight, is spiritually always a great snake, measuring several meters long. When you notice a horse trotting down the road that freezes when a snake crosses his path, the horse will not continue on, it remains standing still, for as long as the small snake passes by with its spiritual length.

Why is this so?

It is because horses have a sense within them that no other species has.

It is never good to kill a snake. As soon as it is killed, its killer undergoes a punishment. He who kills a snake draws upon himself the wrath of other snakes, and snakes are guardians of houses, land, skyscrapers and cities. They are found in the foundations of all buildings and there is a clearly marked cross on their head. The snake guardians of our home are always entered by one soul from our ancestors, to watch over the house, which is inhabited by the present members of that particular lineage.

Without this guarding, there is no life.

Immediately, when the guardian snake of a house leaves, someone dies in that house. Snakes love the sun and from its splendor draw their secret power. There are also snakes that serve evil. These are clearly recognizable. They are poisonous, and they should be left alone and not hunted down. Someone who has been bitten by a venomous snake, and dies from the bite, ends up this way because the spies of the underground world have punished him.

I should note that only special people are able to talk to snakes.

Rats carry a significant omen. Should people notice that there are fewer rats in their vicinity, it is a sign of good days approaching. Rats are the embodiment of negative energy. With all that man has made and has available, it cannot suffice to exterminate the rats.

GUARDS OF THE UNDERGROUND WORLD

On April 24, 1990, I was physically lying on the bed, but something simultaneously happened to me in a vision. The ability of speech was taken away from me, but my brain was functioning normally. There were guardians with me, protecting me from the spies of the underground world. Suddenly the guardians hastened me, warning:

—*They are coming!*

I felt them.

The guardians set fire to all the lights, because the underground spies would flee from them. While in the dark, Evil has power. I walked the rooms looking for a possibility of rescue and then noticed an ancient carriage with six harnessed black horses. The carriage raced at a trot. The Evil was gone.

I was told: on the right side of the body is a positive energy and it is the guardian of every man or woman. On the left side is negative energy, streaming under the left shoulder blade on the back, entering the human body. Forever lurking on the individual, it wants to draw a person into its claws of negative energy.

When a child is born, three women bend over his cradle and determine his destiny. There are three kinds of cradles, and they are all invisible to the human eye. These are cradles for an ordinary, middle and God-given person.

On Earth, no two children are ever born at the exact same moment, in the same split second. Everyone is always born completely alone, as one and unique.

Out of those three women who decide the human destiny, two are good and the third one is a servant of Evil. If the evil one approaches the child first and decides on a difficult destiny for him in his human life, the good ones may mitigate it with their gifts. But if the two good ones approach first, the third evil one may afterwards worsen everything with her endowment.

That is why many give into crime to become thieves, criminals, and murderers in their lives. Negative energy prevails over them, thanks to that evil Judge. Such children, once they grow up, are generally not bound to solid marital relationships, they are not given human birth or those born are bound to evil in advance. In this way, a link in the chain of one lineage splinters, and the entire chain is disrupted.

From the second cradle, as I said, is a person who will live a middle life.

Later in life, they will be tied to politics, but also included are kings, rulers, doctors, scientists, all those who have greater power than the people from the first cradle.

In this second cradle, there is ample work to be done by the Judges, who deal out the destiny for the duration of the lifetime. In their lives, those individuals who have the most success are the ones whose destiny was assigned by the evil Judge, between the two good ones.

But this happens rarely, so the vast majority of people from this cradle end up where all others do who get blood on their hands during their lifetime. Only a few people in this cradle manage to assemble a crown of Good.

In the third cradle, lie the children who will become the messengers of the people. This invisible cradle is all in flowers; fairies and the good spirits of good people protect it. It is in eternal brightness. Very few newborns come to lie in it.

Those who nonetheless find themselves in it are destined for great deeds when they grow up, and Evil is forbidden to access this crib. Whichever child lies in it is immediately placed in heaven. The Divine eye is ever watchful upon this cradle, and also later in life, for these chosen ones. There are very few such exceptional people.

Thus, it has always been.

However, along with the three women Judges who assign the lifetime, everyone is given a Fate. He is the one who sees and evaluates everything, and if need be, may also mitigate the evil which has been cast by the third woman Judge, if she approached last.

This Fate comes around the world every five years, visiting people, entering the house and observing how lives are led. If he concludes that someone has atoned enough for what the third woman Judge has assigned to him, Fate sends his forces to mitigate the misfortune, or end it altogether.

When Fate goes on watch every two astral months, which is five human years, he evaluates what people have been doing in the meanwhile, and he first passes the guards, who give him detailed reports on each individual.

Namely, everything committed by a mortal is written down in the book of life, between the two comings of Fate. Based on the guard's report, the person is judged immediately. Thus all is brought forth, even that which has been unseen by people as witnesses.

There is a well-known saying: the Earth has sworn to the Heavens that all the secrets will be known.

It is true.

It comes true in the following way: Every village, city and street, everything has three guards who are constantly holding vigil and safeguarding. When a thief goes to steal or when someone is killed, without any witnesses around, it seems to the perpetrator that no one has seen anything.

However, all that is done is seen by these guards. Nothing can escape their eyes and their task is to make sure that, even without witnesses, the whole truth comes out sooner or later.

THE CURSE PUNISHMENT

I was given to see:

There was water in the tunnel at Miramarska Street in Zagreb. On one side of it stood an army and on the other side was Freedom. Then, two souls came up from the grave. One was 600 years in the grave, and the other about 300 years.

They said:

> —*The time has come for the removal of the curse. The time has come for realizing who we are, and how we and our sisters have killed and enveloped many people in black.*

The longest curse punishment, which can be given to a country, is 20 astral years. An individual may be sentenced up to 35 human years, which is 14 astral months.

After the expiry of these curse penalties, a human or a country will be given over entirely to negative energy or else the curse is forgiven. Everything depends on the behavior during the curse.

There is always one continent on earth under ice, but it is not always the same one, because this is how it must be. The ice is tied to a curse and its punishment. Soon, a disease will appear, which will ravage for a long time, with no antidote for it, yet.

The new civilization will be created; its time of creation is drawing near. This new civilization will appear in the bright light of the sun, for it will result from it. I have seen details about it, but I will not reveal them because it is not appropriate to the time of purifications, which is taking place now.

Before the new civilization comes forth, there will be great droughts and starvation. When these plagues will stop and when their punishment will be abolished will all depend on people.

There will not be any awakening until man realizes that he should not interfere with nature, for it is godly. Likewise, people must feel the wrath upon their own shoulders, so that they cease penetrating the depths of the earth, for by doing so they are getting closer to the underground kingdom, and the closer they get to it, the more infectious diseases and other assaults will be released out of the earth.

All adversities, accidents and troubles come from the graves of the underground spies, and are the punishments for what ancestors have done or what the individual does now, and this is why descendants may have to atone.

Sinful individuals are punished with a curse, and the seal on that curse signifies the degree of negative energy. A curse on a person as a punishment may be administered from seven levels. Those on the seventh are the most severe and dangerous.

Each of us reincarnates seven times, and thereafter leaves the physical world of people forever. All together, the family name and lineage carries 49 degrees or removals or generations, and then it dies out and as such, disappears.

If all the generations succeed to live decent lives without any punishments, which is extremely rare, the entire lineage moves higher, to again pass through another seven levels. As I stated, such progressions are rare, because just as a man has however many wrongs from his ancestors, so he himself sins for his own descendants in the same lineage.

Negative energy attacks women more often, for women bring offspring into the world, and so negative energy working through them can more strongly affect the physical world of people.

There are many curses, according to how an individual is to be karmically punished, but the most severe are the ones for the shedding of blood in the family and murder. These are the curses that cannot be removed by any means.

A curse does not only involve the individual person. It may engage his entire lineage, which is all of the 49 generations, but it may also encompass the entire country, continent or planet.

The most dangerous time for every person is between 5:00 and 8:00 o'clock in the morning. Because of this, whoever can, should wake up before 5:00 o'clock.

Black magic envelops a person throughout the entire night, but should it be caught while at work come the morning, while the person still sleeps, it falls into him. The Sun will seize it, whereas, it prefers to suck on an individual.

If you do not get up before 5:00 o'clock, you often feel weakened, a headache, or pressure in the chest and head. The place where it hurts is the place through which the energy of black magic is entering your physical body, while you are trying to defend yourself with what is within you, in your physical world. From every human, black magic may exit by means of excrement, and as it leaves it is noticeable by its foul smell of that which decays.

I was given to see:

Marital couples that do not have children are deprived of offspring because a Spirit guide in one of the former generations has been cursed and punished. Only when the curse and punishment pass, may the following generations give birth in that lineage.

But, this does not mean that there are no souls, of those who are to be born, flying above the childless couples. As they approach the woman that should become their mother, these souls are caught and locked into a box that no one can open. These boxes are hermetically sealed containers. These are all taken to the top of a completely impregnable tower and stored there in halls that are alike to great tombs.

THE TIME OF PURIFICATION IS COMING

Nature is now dormant.

First the purification must occur, and then she will wake up.

An ordinary mortal cannot see the invisible world around him with his physical eyes, unless this ability has been given to him. That is unless he is given the power to do so. Soon, people will discover how much wrong they have done, and they will begin to be sorry. But, regardless of this remorse, no one will be forgiven and everyone will have to bear their own share of the punishment.

The time in which we live is a time of changes, purifications. I tell people because I have been instructed to do so; that the days of negative energy's reign are numbered. After the battles comes the purges, which have been set in motion, and then comes the time of the new civilization.

Negative energy comes across as a punishment, which is assigned to individuals for what they or some of their ancestors have done, especially if they have not atoned sufficiently for the deeds committed.

Punishments for any evil committed are great, but cannot last longer than 7 generations within the same family lineage. Once the curse and the punishment are over, a child is born into the world, who has been given birth even before the punishment started.

If there are no instances of breaking any of the Divine laws throughout the seven generations or degrees within a lineage, then after the seventh generation an individual is born who is clairvoyant and who may prophesize.

The purification will be great and far-reaching, people will die and perish, but not from bullets and warfare, rather from famine or absurdly—obesity.

I also owe an explanation: on my astral journeys, one day is equal to the length of one human month in the physical sense.

That is why I also publish:

Negative energy no longer has any business being here; people have changed, and the ruler of the underground world must move to a different planet. Our Earth is facing a great purification. Once it is complete, total harmony and felicity will arrive.

The longest a man may live is for three astral, or spiritual years, and at the end of each astral year, he is judged for what he has done in the meantime, but also for the way he endures the punishments he was adjudged in the meantime.

Overall, a life spans up to 100 of our human years. But, what about those individuals who live longer? When the length of their life exceeds the allowed limit of a human life, it is the result of a mistake in the making of their candle of life.

Every 7,500 human years, God, who created all things, conducts his purges, separating the wheat from the chaff among people. That which is good is left and all evil is destroyed. People perceive this as destruction against each other, but it is actually an invisible divine action.

Purification generally takes the form of wars or epidemics.

Our planet is not alone in the universe, but closely connected to the universe. Visitors from outer space are constantly coming to us.

The majority of them most often come around Siberia, where there once lived a nation that wanted to act like God, and so their country was made icebound as a punishment.

But, since the duration of the punishment is nearing an end, the ice has already started to melt and is decreasing, until it vanishes completely in the future. In the depths of the Earth: there are many wonders that the human eye will never see or explore, because the power of humans is but a drop in the ocean of divine power.

In the interior of the earth is the underground kingdom. From here, from the eternal darkness, in the dead of the pitch-dark night, Evil comes out on the surface of the Earth and rides across the world in its black carriage, pulled by six harnessed black horses, spreading negative energy.

Darkness is its natural environment, and what it hates most is love.

THE CHAIN OF LIFE

In order to explain the chain of life, I must say something that some will understand and some will not. The circle of life is always a connected chain, and links may break within it, when the negative underworld works in one chain.

I will give a more detailed explanation, so you can be the judge and decide.

Have you ever asked yourself the following:

Why does a mother love her son so much?
Why doesn't a mother-in-law like her daughter-in-law?
Why does a father love his daughter so very much?
Why doesn't a mother-in-law like her son-in-law?
Why does the son love his mother, and daughter her father?

These are all reincarnated figures. It means that in the previous life, the younger son was actually his own father, and the daughter was the wife in a former life. So, it all continues in the form of a chain, only in the bodily world a person cannot feel it because this ability is not given.

These are the links, which go on, and life resumes in a chain-form. All human life passes in circles. We are all divided according to ancestry and as life reincarnates, we are just the reincarnated characters of our ancestors.

Life is a chain, which continually goes on, and every link is very important.

This chain of life may break only when the negative energy becomes involved. On earth, there are always a certain number of people and this number never changes. Neither does it decrease, nor does it increase.

As many as are born, so they die.

In my visions I have seen myself lying in bed with my mother, and then suddenly I see my wife, so I asked my Spirit guide if this was possible.

> *—Yes, it is possible. Your father and your mother, it is you and your wife, but in a previous life.*

For all these questions, you bring your own jury, so judge for yourselves. This time, a mother loves her son as someone to be raised in her emotional life, and her husband in the physical, emotional and love life. So, this is where the link continues on, and again I say, life goes on, that is life after life.

Actually, new life is created.

Reincarnation takes place both with humans as well as with plants, just as it does with animals, and actually with everything that breathes the spirit, all is reincarnated.

Given that many people have asked me about this, I can say that I perceive reincarnation as life after life.

There have been a lot of cases where a person comes to an unknown place, but once there, everything seems so familiar. He recognizes something, which he could not have heard about from anyone.

And so we say, life after life.

A person really recognizes all those places where he once lived, and what is more, he could manage to find the money, a treasure, that was once buried in his previous life.

Science would say that these are phenomena, and I claim that there is no phenomenon. This was a mistake while erasing the previous life, where there was a failure to delete everything, and so the past life appears in this life.

So, everyone lives many lives.

MANKIND IS ASLEEP

Mankind has been caught in a great drowsiness.

Yes, humanity is asleep, and the deceased souls, which both help and harm are always with us.

When you go to the cemetery, I advise you not to walk around in it. When you go at least once a year to visit your deceased ones who have been buried for years, symbolically take flowers, wreathes and candles with you. Do not take anything from the graves.

When you arrive, you must obligatorily light one candle, not on behalf of the soul you came for, but for all the known and unknown souls.

This is the only way to defend yourself from the attacks of negative energy.

Light the second candle to the deceased for whom you have come. Please, initially realize that the cemetery may be several hundred years old, and people are there from past times, buried and wandering the cemetery. Those you came for now receive the flame and the ransom, whereas the rest have not received any light because of great hatred and selfishness, and no one illuminates them. You have the opportunity to do this, but out of great ignorance, you do not do so and then the deceased want revenge. You come home and the house is a hell and chaos arises, as on All-Hallows Eve and on Remembrance Days.

If you are already planning to go to visit your deceased in their resting place, then you should do it with dignity. You should first light a candle to all the departed souls, which now wander, and you will see your good fortune rise to the sky.

And you will say to yourself:

—*Why would I light a candle, when I don't even know them?*

This is selfishness.

Have you not asked yourself who will light a candle for you when you are dead?

Please, let this be an explanation and a warning:

First, never take anything from the cemetery back home. Second, do not be selfish when you arrive; light a candle for those departed. Third, light a candle flame for those dearest to you, and then you will receive peace from all these departed souls, who have been pursuing you.

And, so the deceased will help you in the future.

The human souls of the dead are all around us. Sometimes, we can see them when they take the form of some birds like a sparrow or a titmouse, but they are usually invisible to human physical eyes.

Deceased souls can see everyone.

Those who belong to the underworld, who have returned back to make some kind of evil, can see them. They would be able to view the deceased at midnight and in the evening around 8:30 p.m. This regards the deceased who have, during their lives, gone and joined the underground world. The reason they come back is to do what they did not have time to do during their human life. These are people who have worked with black magic and nothing is sacred to them. This is why their souls keep returning back, seeking forgiveness, or to finish what they were unable to do during their previous lifetime. These deceased souls seek redemption, but cannot find it until they are forgiven and led towards the eternal resting place.

DO THE DECEASED HELP US?

I answer the following:

—They can!

When someone comes to me wearing black, I ask them:

—Why do you wear black?

At that point, many do not understand. They generally answer:

—My father died, or my child, or my mother.

Now I will say the following and you are the judge of it:

—By wrapping yourself in black, you are engulfing yourself. You attract evil to yourself. You bathe in tears, but you cannot bring the departed back. You suffer, lament and even harm yourself.

I know this is unclear to you. You directly push this deceased person, who was very good, into the underground world, and you do not allow them to get out of there.

Why?

Because they cannot see you during this time, for you are in the dark, and we know that darkness and light do not go together. You also push them away whenever you are continuously in tears.

How can they help you when your tears are so powerful that their soul, willingly or unwillingly, drowns in your very own tears. For a

218

tear from the eye is something most pure. As they flow like a river, you are not aware that they are destroying your health and your life.

You are not even aware of how much you are disrupting the deceased one's resting place, and therefore drag them straight towards the underworld ruler, for by your lamenting and suffering, they actually cannot see you. This means that at this time, you cannot help yourself precisely because you are in darkness.

Once, in a vision, a deceased child told me:

—*You can see me Uncle Ivica, go to my parents and tell them that I can no longer lie in my resting place for they have cried over me so very much and still do. It is all wet.*

This was a great surprise, so I went to the father and mother of that child and asked:

—*Has your child really died?*

The people told me:

—*Yes.*

So I explained:

—*Your youngster told me that if you do not stop crying and rejecting him with darkness, you cannot help him. You are jeopardizing his resting place, and secondly, misfortune will soon befall your other son. A dog will bite him.*

I told them that if they accepted this, their other son would remain alive in this life.

Please, when I came to this family, the people did not know me. Even I was surprised that everything happened just as this deceased boy had told me it would. The dog did break loose and the accident should have happened, but as you can see, the other son remained alive.

With this example, I want to draw your attention not to cry too much for the dead. Try to realize all this, despite how painful it is; understand that no one can ever change destiny. Destiny may be mitigated, but it cannot be changed. I hope you understand what I have told you, and now know that the departed may help or hinder.

I would like to go back a bit into the past:

As a boy, I saw three people, all deceased, walking the street in the span of 6 months. I am one hundred percent certain that these two old ladies and a girl were deceased. They were led by the girl, walking arm-in-arm along the way, to the home of the deceased.

That was very strange and extraordinary to me.

I asked my family members whether they saw them, but no one did, except for me. I also tried to explain it to someone else, other than my mother, but was ignored, laughed at and persecuted. No one saw them.

Well, that was my life.

So, the departed help. Not in the physical, but in the spiritual world, and as much as you want them to. Understand, the spirit is so close to humanity since man is also spirit. Spirit and matter make up life on Earth. The spirits of the deceased both help and harm.

CHAPTER 7

BARRIERS ON THE PATH

NEGATIVE ENERGY

People are most interested in my prophesies about the future and in protection from negative energy. You all know that I am an ordinary person; I do not differ from ordinary people in any form, but I do have an energy which gives me the power to speak about this and protect all who turn to me asking for my help.

Negative energy never rests. To every positive creation, it responds with negative vibrations. Money is negative energy. Evil is generated easily over money, it multiplies and the number of people with negative energy grows. Actually, they spring up like mushrooms after a rain. But, just as every mushroom lasts for a short while, negative energy likewise lasts for a short span and quickly disappears.

This is particularly true of false prophets and fake healers who also have negative energy, and their only goal is to catch people in their dark traps and to get as much money out of them as possible. In order to be successful, they sometimes actually foresee something true or heal someone, but only to deceive people with their evil charms. I cannot describe it in different terms than the survival time of a mushroom, and it is easy to comprehend this as far as human time.

Murderers are great sinners. Anyone who kills in order to get rich is an eternal servant of negative energy.

Regardless of whether someone kills in war, as a necessary self-defense, in negligence, or as a result of a loss of awareness, the killer must always do his spiritual sentence of punishment.

Anyone who accidentally kills another in a car accident has undergone the same event, but with reversed roles, in one of their past lives. Those charged with negligent homicide are always paying for a karmic debt of the past.

It is tit-for-tat, and thus the sin is atoned.

Why, however, do innocent victims fall?

Those who are innocent, and yet still get killed, come to die only because they were caught between the positive and negative energies. In one of their next lives, the situation will be reversed, and the victim will be the killer in order to redress the balance.

Why does bloodshed happen?

It is because the earth must drink in the blood, for it is the food for the servants of the underground world. For these underlying reasons, wars and mass murders hold the greatest concentration of negative energy.

Negative energy can transform into any character.

The underground world selects the deceased souls that will work for it and gives them power.

Before the activities of black magic begin, the spies from the underground world check the home they want to harm for any positive energy. Also, if there is none at all; did anyone once steal, did someone kill another, or was there infidelity in the house, violence or any other misdeeds.

As soon as it is established that the house is under a curse of punishment for the crimes committed, the negative energy may enter it freely and take it over in its entirety.

Among the members, it chooses the victim most right for the purpose and through this person, as a suitable medium, it works on all the others.

Two deceased females, whose spirits are allowed to do evil exclusively, especially amplify the effect of negative energy. One of them pulls into the navel and the other into the heart of the chosen victim. The person will feel a twinge in the chest, unaware that the negative energy is already within.

Of these two deceased women that have crept into the human body, the one that draws into the human heart is more dangerous for she can cause a heart attack. This soul from the grave sticks needles, like a fish bone, into the inner organs of the human body, whose reflection is in the outer aura.

Such a needle must be cast out of the physical body through the mouth, because it is here that she entered the physical body from the spiritual side while the person was asleep.

Until it is ejected, the individual falls ill with disease caused by this black magic.

Individuals that are entered by negative energy become nervous, quarrelsome and irritable. They start to drink, fall ill, and may even end up as a murderer or go insane. It all depends on the amount of negative energy that is received.

Here is how negative energy works in the house. A married couple with their own children, who were happy until recently, suddenly have quarrels arise at home. Intolerance appears, and the house remains without a blessing.

THE MALE WORLD OF NEGATIVE ENERGY

Most often, I am asked how to identify people with the power of negative energy, and how they affect ordinary people.

I have said that both men and women deal with black magic, but I have not told how they can be recognized, so I will explain.

First, I will start with how to recognize the men who work with negative energy. Initially, I must say that men are more dangerous than women. Please, bear in mind that there are very many of those who work negatively, but in different ways.

I will start with a man, whom the negative energy draws in during the early days of youth. They and like people work through their eyes. They have distinctly blue eyes, are skinny, and live to a very old age. This kind of man must have a twin, both being male, but they are not even aware that they are negative.

They work negatively because one of the two is returned to his mother's breast. This child is originally weaned from his mother's breast, but due to a great illness, his mother brings him back to suckle. At the time when his mother returned him to breastfeeding, an evil spirit entered and remained within him.

Such children are called returnees.

They have a negative effect on their environment, both in the neighborhood and in their own house.

We feel this in the following way:

Whenever such a child sees a woman, a cow or any other animal that has given birth, he cuts the newly born life with his eyes and thus works in this way, always negatively. They do not know how to do anything, yet they cannot bear to watch something that is procreated. They affect everyone negatively, and we need to keep guard for these and similar people.

This is one example of how negative energy can affect the normal world.

Another example relates to a man who has a special legacy of power from a grandmother with knowledge of witchcraft. When she feels her time of death approaching, she transmits this onto her grandson.

The grandmother conveys this power to him so that he might continue with the work that she has done during her own lifetime.

She can only grant this to a male child, and the child must always be the son of her son.

When this grandmother dies, her spirit will always hover above that grandchild, driving him to do evil.

This man may be recognized in the following manner:

His physical stature is short and he has lighter hair, and is quite stocky. He must actually be very stocky, if not fat, and appears unfriendly. He always breathes deeply and when nothing works, he sighs. He can take what he wants with the help of his deceased grandmother's spirit, for the power she once had moves instantly into this man.

He can do anything that is negative.

These people and people like this attack material assets the most; they take away a cow's milk and are very capable with their land. Their acreage is always more fruitful than the neighbors. If such a person works in a company, he always receives a higher salary than anyone else working in the same position.

People like this act only for their own interests. They accumulate much material wealth for themselves; they become widowed at an early stage, and always encounter great problems with their sons. Fights are ever present in their home. A person like this considers himself a great man, and he can affect ordinary men for his own personal gain.

The third kind of people to stay away from appear rather intoxicated, somnolent. When an individual comes across them, one feels afraid. These men know precisely how to treat and adapt to any environment in which they find themselves. They work very negatively and are skinny and bearded. They have long fingers that are very elegant, and work strictly with gloves on.

They feel they have been given a natural gift, and begin to exploit what they have been given. Bioenergy is the first sign that leads these people to the realization that they possess something more than ordinary men.

For example, such a man goes to his car and sees sparks flashing from his hands. He realizes that this is bioenergy, and since money is his greatest lust, he begins to supposedly help people. When such a person sees his rising success, he quickly decides to materialize them and charge for these services.

This person then notices that he is losing his power, without realizing he has been tested. As soon as he accepts money and gives up charity, Satan enters into him. When he sees himself losing those people who were coming to him, he starts to wreak vengeance on those people.

And so all that once was used for good is now turned towards vengeance, and those he once helped, he would now destroy.

Most often, this is done through a picture, where he gets a needle used to sow a cadaver, because this needle is bewitched. Piercing the picture of the victim, he uses this photo to commit this and other orgies that the underworld has given to him and people like him.

This is where those who were once helped start to fall ill, and again come to seek his help. Thus, he resumes drawing money from them.

He commits all sorts of orgies, and this has a very negative effect. Even more, he buries these pictures on a grave, and in so doing no one can ever redeem him. He never again does good, only evil.

We must keep away from these types of people.

There are people who can do both evil and good. In the Muslim world, as with the priesthood in Christianity, a man who works in a mosque is called an imam. These people are trained through the Quran, and know how to do evil and good to a person. If you ask me, the one who does evil cannot also do good. And, of these imams, whoever is doing good, may only do good and he will always work for the benefit of a person.

If an imam chooses, and I mean those working in evil, he can make a person go mad, ensure that a girl never marries, or that a young man never finds a wife, and anything else. And, when he has collected a good amount for these services, then he can send the same person to the good imam, so that the latter removes it.

There are some people who know that they are in this negative circle, and think they can remove the spell themselves. You have to understand me, a person who has never done any wrong to another is the only one who can remove a spell.

I would like to give an example to show you what I mean.

When you go to the market and buy some fruit or meat, once your have paid for this food, it becomes yours, the ransom has been met. You have exchanged money for this food and may freely eat it. You would not be afraid that someone would come to your door and question where it came from. Since you know that you bought it, you eat it freely, without any fear.

The same goes for removing black magic. Whoever takes it away must buy everything back from the underground world. This is how someone frees you from more cursedness and ends the spell.

I give you this example so you may better understand.

There is another thing I have to say here. Any person who deals in this business of allegedly removing black magic, and sends you from pillar to post, and then tells you the price of it all, believe me, you have only thrown your money away. You have not been helped at all, for he immediately charged, placing a wild price on it, and out of this nothing will come.

You must understand that when you come to a person who sees and knows, someone who will not commit a sin by his soul for anything in the world, then tells you that he will remove this for you, do not believe him. When you go to these people, you will immediately recognize them by asking how much you owe them, and they will smile and say:

—*If you can spare something, leave it, if not, just go.*

They know that you will donate as much as you can. And, when you ask them to undo the black magic, and they tell you that they cannot promise anything, but they will try, and then send you off with a smile saying, go, we shall see.... You can trust such people. One's like this have surely helped a hundred percent.

But also be sure upon your success, which came spontaneously, to come back and thank this person. And then because you would like him to, he may accept a gift from you and money. People like this you can feel free to trust.

We still have one last type, and these men are the prophets who foresee the future. They have passed through the greatest difficulties and they are strictly chosen. They have been tried in all areas of life, and those who become such individuals, have all been acquitted.

People like this are not allowed to commit any evil deeds against anyone, they must not kill, they must not think anything bad of anyone, they must not punish, they must not be adulterous, they must simply do everything right. And if they pass all these exams, they first become teachers, just as teachers who teach children in elementary school, and then lecturers, professors, doctors, masters and in the end, rulers. Until now, the one and only man who has become a ruler is Jesus Christ—the King of Heaven.

THE FEMALE WORLD OF NEGATIVE ENERGY

So far, I have spoken about the men, whom we should keep on our guard for; so, now I will talk about the women. Women are much less severe than men, but there are also dangerous ones. The worst of the women are those that cause nightmares.

These are busty, masculine and very miserable women. They come during the night, taking the stock of milk or else come to a person in the form of a nightmare. They come while a person is sleeping, and bind him like an octopus does its prey, and always suck on the person's left breast. This is one kind of woman.

Others are the second kind who have inherited evil from their previous life that they carry inside them, and they deal it away to others by means of various spells.

The third kind are women characterized by possessing "snake-like" eyes. Their acts are very negative, and they can cast spells for a person at home to suffer from intense madness, for great conflict to arise in the house, for fights to break loose, and for the livestock to become sterile. These are the women with snake-like eyes who can cast spells on a person and affect their surroundings.

The fourth kind of women go to the cemetery at night; takes the mortuary earth, bones from the deceased and the water in which a dead person was bathed. Then they throw it on those neighbors who are in better standing than they are, and great adversities begin to happen in the homes where this has been cast. Since I have already written about the great danger of bringing something home from the cemetery, I repeat here that the same case is true, so here the house enters the underworld, and it is very difficult to escape.

Primarily, these women are very dangerous for the neighborhood. They do not work for money, but enjoy inflicting evil, taking revenge, and they are not even aware of why they do it. No one turns to these kinds of women for help, and they are in our everyday lives. We meet them on the street; they behave like ordinary people, but radiate very negatively, just as I have described them.

If you ask me about witches, as we call them here, or sorceresses, I would like to say the following about them:

They also possess a gift, but whenever they would do something positive, controlling it would immediately arise and with that the negative energy would speak through their mouth, and they would start charging, taking money from people, and doing it all for money. In this way, they have handed away their gift to the underground world, and thus get called witches, sorceresses, fortunetellers and frauds.

Woman like this can no longer do good, just like the men taking money who allegedly foresee from coffee grounds, cards and many other means that reflect. I would not advise people to go to these women, but if you go, it will only result in the loss of your money.

Those women who deal with prophesizing destiny are called prophetesses. They undergo the same phases as men do. These prophetesses cannot help, they can only see an individual's destiny and if they have not tarnished themselves anywhere, they may also predict conflicts and wars, earthquakes, accidents and everything positive or negative.

Such women differ greatly from the other types. They do not charge for their work, they truly see and understand that whoever sees must not even think about charging. These and such women are in the first stage of a teacher, then lecturer, then professor. They go on receiving titles, until they become holy personages and then churches, monasteries and temples are erected for them.

Here is how to recognize negative people who are doing harm to others, and we must keep safe from them since the underground world has such a negative effect on people.

This means that anything can be cast upon people.

BLACK MAGIC

Nowadays, people are very interested and convinced that there is some kind of negative force affecting their feelings. This negative energy is the foundation of what we call black magic.

Black magic is mostly practiced in America, where it has the most control. In former Yugoslavia, the most famous for magic are Bosnia, one part of Serbia, Kosovo, Macedonia and Jastrebarsko near Zagreb.

Here, there are great springs of black magic circles.

Apart from former Yugoslavia, black magic is practiced in almost all of Italy, one part of Germany, France (Marseille), Great Britain and a part of Spain and Turkey.

In the countries I just mentioned, black magic governs the most, which does not mean it does not also govern in other countries, just to a lesser degree.

Black magic always serves a negative purpose. It can be identified by the way in which it acts; it targets illness, strife, neurosis, and most often it can target murder. As soon as one notices black magic, one must seek help immediately.

This also involves the deeds of evil women who deal in black magic. Driven by jealousy, she goes to the butcher shop and takes from the butcher's block what she needs, performs her ritual, expertly and professionally, then goes to a house and while the hostess is preparing the guest's lunch, she drops her preparation into this dish.

Once people eat it, negative energy instantly moves into their homes and immediately starts working. Restlessness takes over the house, and what's more, physical assaults arise between the wife, husband and children. Anger, pain, bitterness and unrest prevail in the house. The job is done and people do not know what to do next.

I am describing this as an example, so you may see how black magic works.

Black magic is cold and is transmitted in the following manner: when the wind plays with the leaves, it is transferred from individual houses and may remain in them for eight months of astral life at most, namely 20 human years. Black magic always lasts for an even number of human years.

Whoever has been affected by black magic and has fallen ill or has become disturbed by it may no longer be helped. Neither conventional medicine nor alternative healers with their abilities can offer any help.

Black magic works both spiritually as well as physically, and even more, there is a materialization of certain things. When we say that something is diabolic or that something is not working well, it means that the person concerning this experience has fallen into the underworld.

Witches who come to earth from the underground world in human form must perform black magic by order of the underworld lord; they receive, beforehand, precise instructions of what to destroy in homes, in families or with individuals. As a rule, they perform black magic on homes in which there is no positive energy.

In the house where black magic has been brought, at least one pillow is full of the obvious evidence of witchcraft, and it is surrounded by black magic. Illnesses and fights take place among its members and there is never peace in such a house.

And involuntarily, a person can make a mistake and draw black magic into the space where he lives. This is done primarily by planting certain trees; mainly pine trees, fir trees, box trees and cedar trees. These are the evergreen species, which attract evil spells just as they do evil souls, who wish to harm living people. Specifically, these evergreen species have a substance within them that is tied to cemeteries, so they may only be planted and gardened exclusively in cemeteries. Should these species be planted next to a house, it turns into a cemetery and the aforementioned substance only enhances the activity of the evil spirits of black magic.

Since God no longer helps the people in these houses, they will surrender their power over to the rule of the underground lord, who by means of his spies and messengers, starts affecting them. Houses surrounded by these trees and ornamental shrubs are the first sign of the reign of the underworld spies.

I will give you an example right now. Several months ago, I was away on business, and when I returned, I came back to a waiting room full of people, both men and women among them. As soon as I walked in, I immediately burst out and chased off a woman, about 45 years old, in front of a large number of witnesses. At least one hundred people were standing about when I told her to get out of my sight.

Why I did this, trust me, I did not know. I just said: *Get out! Get out! Get out!*

This woman came with a friend, and her daughter and daughter-in-law were present, but I did not chase off anyone else, only this woman. The woman was so polite, she did not want to argue with me, she only left. As there were a great many people there, I admitted and worked with all the other visitors, including her daughter and daughter-in-law. People scattered, and I did not pay any attention, nor did I ask myself why I chased that woman away.

Now, I will give you the answer, which came spontaneously to me. The next day that same woman came back again and somehow snuck her way in to me. Since all her relatives told her that I do indeed see everything, human curiosity brought her to me again. When she came, I told her in a calm and quiet tone:

—*Well, woman, I already banished you from here.*

She was already seated in a chair. I took in a group of about fifty people, and said:

—*So, I drove you out.*

And she said:

—*Yes, you did, but please receive me.*

I looked into my old mirror and do you know what happened to this woman?

This woman had killed her husband, and for twelve years she has been serving her sentence. Do you know how she killed him? She killed him with her lover, and she chopped him up and put him in the freezer.

Please, after I told her all this, the woman confessed it and she said:

—*It is not that you are a psychic, but a man of God. You really see all and know everything.*

The earthly court of justice has ruled on her, and with God, as you can see for yourself, she has not been tried yet.

In a crowd, I have recognized those people who are very sinful and who have done something. For these and similar people, the court judgment they have received here is not the end, and their real forthcoming trial is yet to come.

And now, I would like to talk about a young man. He is from Zagorje, and his name is Danijel. He came to me over a year ago. I admitted him, talked to him and this young man visited me constantly. He always asked me to do the water for him, the one that I make, and he would always say that he was doing better.

Whenever I worked with this young man, I would always open the door to a large number of witnesses to show them what was actually wrong with him.

This young man is 35 years old, he is a father of three children, is very rich in material terms, and he says he would give away everything he has in this world just to get rid of the animal that is within him.

This all began two months ago. He started shaking a bit and now he shakes like a leaf. I would like to describe this story to you in a bit more detail. As soon as I would call this man and raise my hand in his direction, that animal would start to dance about significantly within him. I fought it with all possible means that I know, to try to open it up, but it could not be opened. Finally, he told me that he saw a chest, in which the animal is kept. This chest is shining and it started to crack, as it is egg-shaped, and it was supposed to break for the animal to come out.

Today, as I was working with him, he told me, in front of a number of witnesses, that he saw a lit candle and suddenly a great cross, and that he could see himself behind the cross. Then, he saw this animal wanting to jump out from the egg-form, but it did not really know where to go. When he is rid of it, this young man will find his peace of mind.

When I finished the session, again I asked him in the presence of my lawyer:

—*Do you believe that you will be helped?*

He said that he did believe, but that he was not psychologically mature enough.

As it stands, somewhere deep in his psyche he feels sorry for it to leave, so in essence, he wants the animal.

He stated further:

—*I've been everywhere, wherever I heard there might be someone who could help me, because this has been haunting me since I was fourteen years old. If anyone else were in my place, they would have gone mad and committed suicide. I have been driven straight to taking my own life, and everything keeps going through my mind and I cannot take it any longer.*

My lawyer asked him why he did not go to the doctor. He said:

—*I have been to doctors and they have all declared me nearly insane.*

Then he continued:

—*I don't go there any longer. I know Ivica will help me, I just need to ask with my heart. Trust me, I still haven't done that, and as Ivica says there are no coincidences and that this is not a coincidence, I most certainly will do so when the time comes to get rid of the animal.*

This is one of my hardest cases and when I solve it, I will surely heal people like this much more quickly than I have been doing thus far. Evil has settled into this young man. This is a very sinister evil. It is biting and eating away at him, and willingly or unwillingly, it will have to come out, and this is the knowledge

241

from the other side of the wall.

Since masses of people come to me, I mention all of this to you so that you are informed. You can see all sorts of people turn to me for help. I am happy when I help people and solve things painlessly, but with this young man, with him the work is exceptionally difficult.

When a person gets a headache, they think it just happened, it aches either because of the flu or a cold. I will not say there are no such cases. There are, but there are some cases where a person lies down, and evil spirits come into play, called sheitans in Islam. They know very well how to stir up and cause confusion in the mind of a person.

A person takes one, two or three aspirins, but his head continues to hurt. Then he feels fear, which is always present, and this leads to great anxiety. Nerves get frayed, the person retreats into himself and feels haunted by something negative, and so I also admit such individuals.

If you could see the joy in these people whose heads have ached them into exhaustion. They were afraid of going into traffic, afraid of the dark, afraid of everything. They say that when I touch them with my hands, they are like new and look forward to tomorrow.

I work with these people by killing the negative with that which radiates from my hands. This irradiation that shines from my hands does not feel good to the negative world, the world of the underground.

And so it leaves with its unfinished business, and great peace takes over. In places where the aura is broken, I bind it back together, then I make and set a circle, and thus remove the blockage.

The spirit that was present here, the sheitan's spirit, was repeatedly burned and fled. These are the so-called local or bad frequencies. These treatments are very brief and resolve very quickly. When this regards headaches, nervousness, pain in the legs and in the back, this is dealt with in great swiftness. The negative force cannot act, and is therefore, promptly driven away.

I have repeatedly said that black magic exists and is present in our everyday lives. It comes easily, and it is very difficult to get rid of it.

I would advise everyone not to get involved in the orgies of black magic, and when you hear that some kids are conducting these orgies, performing some rituals, leave it alone. These individuals are undisciplined and irresponsible.

They are not aware that on the day of their orgies and acts, their group actually enters the underground world.

As I said, black magic is easy to cast, but much harder to resolve later. Drug addicts and alcoholics are an example here. For these people who end up living their lives in this way, the life span is short, and they no longer have any purpose in this worldly life.

Negative energy does not create a man.

Drugged and drunken people see the beauty that comes especially from the underground world. I say this because it draws the children, between 15 and 18 years of age, so I advise parents to make sure that this does not happen to their children. Everything short-lived, and all that does not last for long, is given from the underground world and we must strictly guard ourselves from it.

The underground world has never worked as publicly as it has for the past 40 years. Negative energy has made a great sweep and is destroying everything it can get its hands on. I have already stated that its orgies are coming to an end. It now feels like a drowning man clutching at straws, because it knows it must leave this planet. No one else will defeat it, for only God can do so.

God never punishes man out of hatred, only out of love, because God created man out of love.

Black magic works in many ways. If people only believe in money, it means they are spiritually absent. Then, black magic gains momentum, which is visible in our world, as it has led us to where we are today. The underground world is so strong that only God can save the people from it.

ST. GEORGE'S DAY

In a year, the most dangerous date lies between May 5th and 6th, before the dawn of Saint George's day. I would like to tell you in detail what I have been given to see and know. What is the actual significance of St. George's day, and why do the so-called witches, magicians and the underground world have the opportunity at this time to cast evil upon a person that can last for the entire human year?

I will explain in detail. As I have written many times about the Gypsies, they are a nation which is the oldest in this civilization. It is scattered throughout the entire world, and finds its peace everywhere, always cheerful and always dynamic. It is a nation that does not have its own ruler, a nation that does not have its own state, these are our Gypsies. Among the Gypsies, one of them was St. George. Why do they call him a saint? He is a saint because on the day of May 5th, he came to a forest in the mountains, where he was attacked by a great dragon, a big beast which he had to fight. This battle went on for the entire night until the dawn of May 6th. This period, while he fought with the animal, is a time of penance and this time is traditionally left unprotected. Before dawn, as the sun rose, the dragon was killed and Gypsy George became the victor.

Gypsy's celebrated this glory, because he had killed a great evil that was attacking them. Since then, it has remained the tradition for St. George's day to be celebrated, and all Gypsies; Orthodox, Catholic, and Muslim, all celebrate this day, offering a sacrificial lamb as a great sacrifice for their St. George.

That is why they have taken this day and celebrate it, while black magicians attack and bring vengeance to people during this time. George managed to kill the beast with a hornbeam rod and blackthorn stake.

Black magicians only have power during the time while the beast was fighting for life and death, and when the Sun rises they no longer have any. Whatever they do during those nightly hours is all the time they have. If they cast evil on a house or on livestock, this house will be in a severe imprisonment for the entire year, and I do not know who can help or when help may come if the house

245

is not protected from evil.

That is why the house, the barn, and everywhere a person lives are adorned with hornbeam, blackthorn, hellebore and willow tree branches, in order for the dwelling to be safe for the night. When the evil spirit comes to attack the household, these branches that are set around the house prevent it from acting as it would if the household were unprotected.

Here you are, this is the tradition.

When you see people on the evening before Saint George's day adorning their house, keep in mind that they were told by some good people to do so, and therefore, this house is safe.

Hornbeam is placed out because the animal was killed with a hornbeam branch. A blackthorn branch is placed out because the accursed animal's heart was pierced with a blackthorn stake.

Hellebore is used because it is very poisonous to the accursed creature, whose eyesight had a poisonous effect on humans. Willow is used to prevent the placement of something, some kind of spell; as it would cause all to break the way a willow does, so no evil spells would have any effect or be reflected in the house.

A red egg is kept, broken and eaten on the Eve of St. George's day as a symbol of the great days of Easter present in the house.

These are the customs.

People bathe in herbs early in the morning, before the sun rises, so that the whole year will pass by in health, happiness, love and well being.

The herbs would consist of thyme, nettle, willow branches, hellebore branches and hornbeam branches. And, should a girl break those hornbeam branches in the home, boys would grasp onto the girls, respectively girls onto the boys, and as the willow branches break, so would all the evil cast on the house that prevents joy, peace and prosperity. So any harm would break at the same time.

And one speaks:

The left hand is not christened, let there be no spells in this house. The right hand is christened, let there be joy and happiness and luck in this house.

These are the words that are spoken on this day in order to protect the house, and to ensure child bearing and birth.

On St. George's day, spells can be cast that make a person go insane.

Thus, to do this, when someone wants the black magic to work, at night they take one of the conical frames for stacking hay and straw, and this is then twisted: the bottom is turned upwards, and the top is turned downwards, and hairs from the black magician's chosen pray are stabbed into it. The man or the woman then has severe headaches in this unprotected house, and is driven to insanity.

I say again, as long as the house and its residents are unprotected, naked as the day they were born, both men and women who practice black magic come. And, if there are many sheep in the neighborhood, they take a bit of milk, and also dew from the field, a branch of a fruit tree from the orchard and a vine branch from the vineyard. They next bury the vine branch in their own vineyard and the fruit branch in their own orchard, and give the milk to their own stock and smear it on them. And all that happens throughout the year will only benefit those who have taken these items into their own homes.

Then such people watch all their things growing throughout the year, while the other person who is working has everything dry up, becoming devastated and barren. The cows or sheep would nurse, but there would be no milk, the vineyard would run dry and there would be no grapes, and the fields would take off but there would be no yield from them.

He would ask himself; dear God, why does my neighbor have so much and I do not? How is it possible that he is better off than me, when I used to also have it good in my fields, vineyard, orchard, stable and house, but now they are not fruitful?

This is all done on St. George's day, during the time when the animal fought George, because it had power at that time. This much I wish to say about St. George's day, and what dangers lurk and are attempted before the breaking of dawn on that day.

I would like to still say a few words about Gypsies, about the people who do not know that they come from God, that they are Divine, and that God loves them. Gypsies have no country and no ruler.

Tell me, have the Gypsies ever fought a war?

Well no, and that is why they are loved by God. And, why would a Gypsy go to war when God gave him the entire world, so wherever he goes, he is always welcome and always finds his way.

But, their curse is drawing to an end, and a dwelling will be made for them in the near future. They will have their own country, their own rules, their own history and their own civilization. They do, indeed, deserve it.

So much about the Gypsies, and if you ask me whether there are dangerous ones amongst them, of course there are. There are those who belong to the Chergars. Chergars are the most dangerous tribe, which is indeed greatly subjected to the underground world. They know a lot about black magic, they are indeed negative and not good. I am not saying they are all like this, but every wheat has its chaff.

NIGHTMARES

I consider it important to acquaint my readers with nightmares. Nightmares come to their victims and explicitly suck on the left breast of men and women. Nightmares are a somewhat different case than black magic.

A nightmare does not come every night, but only at the times when it knows exactly how much juice it can suck out of the chest of the selected person. Nightmares are conducted by women whose breasts are tremendously large, for it is in them that they store the juice, which they pass onto the person to whom they submit. And, they are very tied to the underground world.

The person who has a nightmare appears very exhausted and terrified the next day, and the nipple on the left side of their chest is noticeably withdrawn.

This is the nightmare; the person can be recognized by their large chest, they appear very manly and serve a different purpose to other people. They are not aware that they have entered the underground world, and they are not conscious that they go out to persecute and harass the human spirit.

It can be assembled in a way that someone must dissolve these nightmare's spells. Apart from the spies, the messengers of black magic, the underground world sends the nightmares to this world of physical people. They especially like to attack men.

This is a woman, otherwise alive and existing physically in this world, who has her own family. She is identified by large breasts, a masculine face, a manly walk and fertility. While her husband is generally skinny and henpecked, he also drinks a lot and inescapably has great problems in his everyday life.

This physically living woman is unconsciously a servant of the underground world. She is not at all aware of what she is doing with her spirit on select nights. She is ruled by negative energy and her task is to suck out a particular juice from the nipples of men. She transmits that juice into her own breasts.

A nightmare arrives every three human months, or four times a year. There is nothing characteristic about her behavior in physical life, although a clairvoyant individual may discern her in a mass of many people. When she is in an encounter with a man, during her dangerous task, he grabs onto her neck and pulls it. Thus, such an unaware servant of the negative energy is able to see bruises on her physical neck and other traces of strangulation, although she is unable to explain how these came about, or who it was that caused them.

In fact, anything that she does as a spirit of the underground world at night is erased from her memory in the physical world. She generally does not even know that she is governed by negative energy. Instinctively, she stays away from people who are charged with positive energy. She avoids and runs from them in physical life without being aware of why she does so. There are unsightly forces of Evil within her, which erase all the evil deeds that she commits from her memory.

I have already written how the most dangerous women are those who have given birth in their life, and had to die at a young age. They are dangerous as they keep returning back to their house, and they are also dangerous for the neighborhood.

They return to the house where they passed away, and just as we go for lunch, they must also come on a daily basis without the victim knowing it. They feed here and resume having a tremendously negative effect on the entire surroundings.

I must mention that this deceased soul never comes alone. She always brings two other deceased souls and together they perform, what we call, black magic. There is great unrest in the house where they return, and no one gets along with anyone. The landlady of the house suffers from severe back pain and her spine begins to contort. This is the way in which they work, and so I advise to never take anything from the cemetery and bring it home.

WHO CAUSES OUR MISERY

Black magic cannot be practiced by anyone if it has not been given them to do so. It is only present in those selected, and so we call such people magicians, witches, sorceresses, and everything that has a negative effect comes from the underground world. We have already said that the world of the underground has a very negative effect on this earthly world.

When we see that everything comes to a sudden stop and that someone is spiritually deteriorating, physically suffering and withering, we immediately know that someone is obviously behind it all. Such a patient would go for a medical examination, and take the medications prescribed by his doctor. The condition would not improve in any way. Then, that man would seek help in alternative healing from those who foresee destiny, who read fortunes from a coffee cup, who perform witchcraft in various medieval ways. There are many charlatans among such people, but there are also genuine prophets.

Magic is generally practiced by women. These women have to possess what the underground ruler has given for them to do and they differ in many ways. Some work negatively by means of nightmares. Others work with certain objects, which are generally taken from graves, a butcher's stump, or the broom used to sweep the house after the deceased has died. Ashes are taken from the place where Gypsies light a fire, also water from three springs at a particular time and they cast magic in this water. For any negative function in which they use things to act, they use everything to their advantage, even the holy water from a church. When all of this has been performed, it is given to the individuals or it is buried in their vicinity for the sorcery to take over the house.

252

In the case where people serving the underground world get their hands on a beautiful girl who is preparing to be engaged, she only needs to agree to marry the groom-to-be who has already arrived, and the joy suddenly ends.

These negative people work by taking a piece of the wedding gown, which the bride is to wear on her wedding day, and bury it on an unknown grave; then the girl would give up on her own destiny and start to atone. She would, for example, choose to be and remain the eternal spinster, and this is where the link is interrupted, which means that the chain has been broken.

All those who cause others evil, suffering, sorrow and bitterness practice black magic. They draw this power from the negative energy of the underground world. All this of which I speak, I can say that I have seen it all because I am permitted to enter and see what is happening on the other side, as well as this side.

No one can practice black magic if he or she has not been given the ability by the underground world. Only with the help of the underground ruler can an individual cast a spell and cause evil to others. Fortunately, true black magicians are actually very rare.

Black magic can only be practiced by women who have already died, but who return from the world of the dead in physical form as a human being, to commit evil. These are very old women, they can even be up to 500 years of age, and are specially chosen. They must have given birth while they still had their own life.

Although, in the likeness of the human creature, these chosen women for black magic are actually spirits from the grave. They most often draw upon feathers where they materialize evil, and commonly weave braids from their hair and feathers to put in a pillowcase.

Also, in these materialized symbols of black magic, they throw in the soil from graves, pieces of gravestones, and even pieces from a casket, bits of burnt out grave candles and an odd number of roasted seeds. All this is placed in the pillowcases, so that the linen is not torn or damaged in any place. This is why nothing must be taken home from the cemetery.

When I said that a broom is used from the deceased person's home, this is how it is done. Depending on how it works and what it does, whether it is for sickness or a great accident, a piece of this broom is tied in the following manner; wood from the cross of an unknown person is taken, and plucked feathers from a chicken, pigeon, canary, or a bird in a cage, and this is tied together. Again, a suitable moment is chosen and this is specially placed in the pillowcase on which the person sleeps.

These and similar things are only done by relatives, who are permitted to enter the house, and are the underground world's sweetest treat. The main cause of all of this are two spirits, the one who was swept by them and the deceased one lying in the grave, and together they go to reclaim what is theirs and settle in. Therefore, these magnets link everything, and the underground world is always present in the house of the person to whom this has been cast upon.

This is one way head related illnesses begin, with major headaches arising. How the underground world is present, I have written here, and the underground world feeds especially on brain cells. It interrupts the flow of blood so illnesses become localized in this area, and it is normal for these individuals to seek immediate medical intervention.

Doctors prescribe strictly based on what science has given them, and the patient keeps suffering from that moment onwards, while the person is not protected, until this is removed or until the designated time of the spell passes.

This is truly very dangerous for the person upon whom this spell has been cast, and may even lead a person to madness. Individuals end up in mental hospitals. This is very dangerous magic.

Men practice black magic in the following manner. These chosen men of the underground world, who are engaged in black magic, usually use a mortuary needle that has been used to pierce a dead man whose shroud was sown with it. When they choose their victim, they most often work through photographs, piercing the most significant places of the person.

Women who practice black magic are initially totally unaware of it, but they unconsciously keep approaching their master with every passing day. When they become aware of what they have done, they regain their consciousness and continue to commit evil deeds.

Please note that these women end up alone, all of their family members abandon them. Once they gain the power, the power of the underground world, they find the greatest satisfaction in planting pine, box, yew, fir, cedar, and all kinds of evergreen trees around their house.

These trees that they plant are vassals of the underground world and grow quickly, filling the area and garden with greenery. It brings misfortune to that house.

I would just point out that these trees always speak:

> —*I am green in the winter and in the summer, and so may my master blacken both in winter and in summer, may this house be wrapped in black.*

When such a tree is planted, either by an ordinary person or a person from the underground world, the house becomes ill fated.

In a rural house owning crops, cows, pigs, sheep, poultry and all that someone keeps to provide food, if the stock starts to die, one can be sure that evil has infiltrated the house and that a spell has been made to target the misery of the landlord.

This is done in the following way.

Someone who hates another person is so jealous that the other has what he does not have, that he takes his revenge on this other person's wealth. Such people go to the cemetery, take the mortuary soil and at two o'clock in the morning make a circle with this soil around the victim's stable, or a circle at the place where crops are cultivated and preserved. The deceased come to reclaim this soil, entering and directly settling into the household of this person.

The wealth is moved straight into the underground world after the ring is made, and as long as the victim does not realize this, the spell cannot be broken. When he goes to see someone to remove it, this other person immediately repeats the spell, now in an aggravated and more dangerous form by plucking hairs and feathers from the stock, and sealing the padlock. Then this person immediately receives all the loot taken from the victim, and the padlock is thrown into a balm of water, in a place where water boils.

Here is one of the most dangerous forms of magic, which targets the wealth of the chosen victim. Black magic is interwoven into a person, and first it dissolves his spiritual part. That is, it enters a person through the umbilical cord to the most sensitive station located in the navel. Here is the spirit of the person, and when this ruptures and becomes putrid, it then reaches to ravage the heart. Once it enters the heart, a person is no longer able to do what is good, and this happens in the following way.

Stench enters the umbilical cord, and by means of it, a man or a woman gives in to alcohol, for correspondingly the lower part of the stomach is tied with a wire and a person is in great agony. Blockage occurs. So one suffers from one day to the next. This creates torment in the body and restlessness in the soul, and anxiety is ever present with these kinds of people.

In the upper part around the heart and the respiratory organs, fish bones are stabbed. These are invisible. It should be clear to everyone that these are invisible to the human eye. This can only be seen by those who have been chosen to help these miserable and poor people by means of their powers. The amount of strength that the chosen person has determines the extent to which they can assist the ill person seeking their help.

HOW TO PROTECT YOURSELF

I have already said that the negative energy is located in the bowels of the earth; that Evil is the darkness and the Good is the light. I have told and speak out about how we should protect others and ourselves.

I advise the following: when you see your neighbor grieving, you should also grieve. When you see your neighbor rejoicing, you should also rejoice. When you see something dangerous happening to your neighbor, do not laugh at him. Just by laughing you have opened your heart to let in great malice, you have opened the door to negative energy that feeds on it.

So the neighbor's cow may die, a child may die and other adversities may occur. Do not rejoice in another's sorrow, for then evil will pass to you. Do not ever call and proclaim yourself to be God-given and suppose you can do things others cannot. Please, you do not have the right to do so.

Should you acquire, as today's science calls it, bioenergy; do not be conceited, because you are not God-given and can never be so. As much as you mature and as much as you advance materially and intellectually, you must realize that someone before you earned it all. This is how the help came to you, perchance from a higher force, I do not know. But, do not underestimate others, for you might regret it. Assets and wealth are in no way a gauge of a person's advancement on his own.

This will serve, as I would generally explain it to you, first hand in how to protect yourselves without anyone's help.

As to other factors, there are people directly bound to the underworld who perform witchcraft. Sorcerers, sorceresses, witches and these kinds of people cast evil on others and transmit it onto you. One must keep safe from such people.

Without visiting people who are engaged in removing spells, who say they have the power, I will tell you that every spell cast by these and similar people lasts only 40 human days. It cannot go on for longer since it needs to be renewed.

Well then, please, when you feel a restlessness creeping into your soul, your life, or your family home, do the following:

Burn incense in your family home at the time of Sun rise and at Sun set. Then light a candle and let it burn.

On May 5th/6th with the break of dawn's Sun, bathe in nettle and hellebore, which you can also put in your home. And correspondingly, let your bath be full of the following herbs and cuttings: thyme, willow (you must break the willow), hornbeam, and place these all in the water along with a few fruit tree cuttings; apple, cherry, plumb, morello. Put it all in the tub and take a bath. Once you have taken your bath, you can let it all drain out to the sewer. By doing this, you can protect yourself for the following year.

Here are the ways and means whereby people can protect themselves from the negative energy that stems directly from the underworld.

I would advise all people who sleep on feather pillows to check them at least once a year. Everything they find in them is related to the aforementioned objects I have spoken about, and it is best to throw them away into flowing water.

The foremost thing I can say is that anyone who turns to a person for help must believe in the person's work, and do as they are advised. Having turned to him, do not mock him. Every person who turns for help and who receives a promise, that everything is being done for their welfare, should know that he will not get help if in return, he is asked for money.

Anyone who expects money cannot help you because that person is obviously leaning towards the other side. Such people are very abject. They get tremendous power from the underground world and they only care about money and nothing else. So they can only make an ill person even more ill, and bring about even worse anguish.

We can protect ourselves from black magic in the following way. Only turn to the chosen person who, upon your approach, does not judge one on the basis of religion or race, but looks equally at everyone as a human being.

Just by coming to such a person, they will know and see how much help one needs, and what protection is advisable. This protection must be safely kept, as it was given by the person who made it, and in the place where it belongs. The protection must be safely kept and one cannot pay for this protection.

This must be understood.

I repeat again, whoever charges for such a service commits evil. This is how everyone can recognize a person that is exclusively good or bad.

CHAPTER 8

THE PATH TO HAPPINESS

NO COINCIDENCES

In the beginning, when I would see something beyond mankind, I would speak about what I saw and tell others about it. However, I was then persecuted and ridiculed. I choked in tears because humanity just did not believe me then. I was called the worst names at that time. I was declared a liar, a swindler and some others that cannot be fathomed.

Please, if we briefly look back at the distant past and to our great future, what did I gain from it?

Was I charging my mother money as she responded like a cobra, like a venomous snake? Whenever I said something, no one would listen, but would respond:

—*He's lying, the crook, he's a liar!*

Again and again, I would have to withdraw into myself. Whenever I tried to say something, I would experience the same thing and have to go through these pitiful disgraces.

As I have said, God forbid that anyone else have the same experience.

Then, I started to gently receive messages in my sleep. While my earthly body slept, my joyful spirit, the spirit of consciousness, always fascinating, led me into a rainbow of colors, and spoke to me about all the times that were coming. When this happened, I tried to describe it to my mother, and to all those around at the time, who would always laugh at me. There were never any comments about all of this, so what could I do but again keep putting a fence around me and withdraw into myself. It remained this way until that day when it all started to come true. And so it continued until I spoke to that lawyer, who was also my first listener. She told me:

> —Mr. Prokić, it will not work this way. You first have to touch upon this in a way deemed worthy by the earthly world, so you will have to prove it rationally.

I listened to her and saw that she believed me. Then, I told her the story of when I came home from my regular work and laid down to rest. How it was not my usual rest, and as those doors opened, it was as if I was physically carried over to the place where everything began. Here, it was said; another two steps and I come directly to my father.

In wonder, I naively asked:

> —Well, am I not the child of my earthly father?

The crown replied:

> —You are, he is your earthly father, and I am your spiritual

father. I have been protecting you all this time, when you were rejected and persecuted by everyone. Now, I have decided to give you 23.5 million people, respectively two billion six hundred and fifty million people.

By a miracle, from my left side I was brought this blond man, whose arrival we are now awaiting on earth. Then, as I gave him that first figure of 23.5 million people, I told him:

—Do not let one single hair from any of these people be out of place. Know that I am above you.

Indeed, at the time and since that time, I have received all of this and have been called his son; I became different. And I have not changed, as you yourselves know.

There, you see how the Heavens help and give to me.

All of this power comes from there; and so you began to follow me, listening to all that I have to say. When I receive messages, they are unclear both to you and to me. They are so clear that they cannot be deciphered at the present time. Yet, as I recently announced, we know that the origin of mankind on Earth lies with milk. Gold protects it, happiness accompanies each one of us every step of the way, prosperity comes directly into the home, the golden key and the God-given day is Thursday.

Well then, why don't we celebrate it?

And when we know that all of this is Heavenly spoken, why do we not respect the Heavens?

I know you will ask yourself:

—Mr. Prokić, how do you manage it all? Why have you not been imprisoned yet?

I owe you an explanation for all this, and so I say; the sugar comes at the end.

Just as God created me, at once my helpers were created too, and I now have to publicly relate all and immediately, loudly and clearly, and thank the police. Since I first began doing this work, the police have been familiar with it. They are mine, and I am theirs. It was in the days of Yugoslavia, when I started all of this work. At that time, a young man named Zoran appeared at my door at Tuškanova Street. The boy was 17 years old and suffered from an issue with his spine. Everyone in the neighborhood knew this well. One day, his mother brought Zoran, and I do not know how she found out about the man who allegedly helps, but Zoran came to me.

I don't know the reason why he had not been operated on already due to the curvature of his spine. Zoran said his mother had taken him everywhere, to all the institutions, until she brought him to Mister Ivica Prokić, where he received help. Believe me, this meant nothing out of the ordinary at the time, and now in a minute you will see that I was at a great turning point. In only a few days, the neighbors of young Zoran came to find out that his pain was gone, and this was also heard by a head official; a person whose name for the moment I do not want to mention. Maybe it is still not yet time.

Our esteemed, divested helper is now directly entering the annals of history. Not only will we read about him, but also our children and the children of our children, and other generations, and they will admire his humanity, his great faith and dignity, and how he entered straight into history.

For now, I will not mention his name because he is much loved and appreciated.

Now, let's begin with our story, which happened between five and six years ago. He found out from his neighbors that their son had been healed. Having his own problems and difficulties, this policeman wanted to turn to someone anonymously for the first time, without anyone's knowledge of it. So he knocked on my door at Tuškanova Street.

What I told him then, he will speak about in the future. What it is that I did for this man, he will also relate. I can only say that I did not know who this man was for a long time. When I later checked why I had not been told who he was, the Heavens said to me:

> —*If we had told you that he was an officer, you would have gotten scared and experienced the opposite effect.*

But, as he had already arrived at that time through Destiny, we became very good friends back then, as we are now. He followed my work very carefully, and since I did not ask the gentleman where he worked, this information did not show up until the fall, until October 1990.

My former neighbors at the time saw the public starting to come, and from great malice began accusing me, and this mass of people. Some black witch near me, who was entirely abusive and accursed, called the police numerous times, over and over again. Her spite was fierce, but I never spoke with her, not even a single word. She produced such hatred towards me, and the same towards you. Believe me, I do not even know her name, may the devil take her away. She is around 40 years old, and we may come to know her name very soon. But, what awaits her. There will not be a place for her even in hell. She sought this out, so she should have it.

Back then, she sent two policemen to lock me up in October 1990. When they arrived the people were very calm; as they are now, so they were then. There were about twenty of them in this apartment where I worked. One of these officers was extremely abusive towards me and wanted to take me to the police station. So, I was quite upset. But when we got to the car, the car would not start.

A voice told me:

> —*Tell them the car will not start, and tell the one to be nicer and to stop abusing you. He is a Serb and near Knin, he shall die on such and such a rock.*

I told him all of this. The Heavens could not calm him down. While the other officer remained silent, this one kept on insulting me. He was angry because the car would not start, and so he finally led me on foot to the police station.

When we arrived, he took my ID and said insolently and arrogantly:

> —*Sit here!*

When I sat down, he continued threatening me about being prosecuted; because he said I deceived people, that I was a crook and a fraud. When he took my ID, I thought that I was a man all alone, and you will see that I was not.

I just told myself:

—*God, if I am really as he describes, let me go to prison, and never come out again. Let me die.*

Please, in just two minutes my savior came. My savior, the man who came to me, whom I called a friend, brought back my ID, and started hugging and kissing me. And so I became loved at the police station.

Well, did God not send this man long ago to pass all the tests before this report was filed? And so I went back to work, cheerfully jogging from Medveščak to Tuškanova Street.

Yes, you will ask if there were people waiting for me?

I walked in on more than 70 people. The people did not leave me, and the officer that had provoked me, just as I had told him, was killed on that rock.

Here, this is how I ordinarily work with the earthly people.

And this is how the Heavens help me.

I wanted to rationally show here that there are no coincidences. As then, so nowadays, I am always talked about with tall tales. Just now, who else but the evil tongues of black magicians filed some charges with the police station, stating how I charge for my services and send the money to Chetniks in Serbia. Please, what money am I charging? Ask yourself and your friends when I have taken money from you? What money could I possibly give away to someone when no one gives me any?

Just as I am spat upon and attacked, the Heavens protect and really help me.

Please, let the esteemed black magicians know that I burn incense in the rooms as well as light a candle. By lighting that candle every working day, I first recover everything that they have just left behind to cause complications for me. And so these things go away to take their mischief elsewhere. These kinds of things today do not find peace anywhere. What they left for me, to themselves these things go back to have their fun. Everything that they tried to plant for me has only been returned back to them, and nothing more. As much as they wanted me to suffer, this is exactly how much misfortune they now watch in themselves. They alone are to blame for having to come to me now for help, for until recently they have used the tricks of black magic to disable me and set obstacles on these, our paths.

But, understand and realize that these are not my obstacles, they are mine and yours, so they are our obstacles.

For the commandeering of my strength, and your strength, and I have already said that you are my strength; you judge these and similar underworld intruders.

I have had the opportunity of meeting these people in my work place, as well as in other locations, and you have the same opportunity. These are the obstacles on the path of life, on the prophetic path.

When you come to me, please do not think that your prophet is without problems, that my life is ideal, that I can do everything and that no one can do anything to me. Please, you are deceived! It is not as you imagine it to be. I also have obstructions, but not as you do. I am the one who eliminates and throws out your obstacles, who cleanses your life paths and prevents you from falling into these and similar problems.

I am sending you to your Life path, to a more beautiful path, towards a better tomorrow and towards brighter times.

THE HEAVENS HELP US

One evening, the Voice told me to be in great concentration alone in my room, without my wife and children, and that it would then inform me of what I should pass on to all of you. It told me:

—*How, what, where, and when all of this comes, you will tell people in your last book.*

And this is what I am doing now.

When I say the Heavens have chosen me and are helping me, do not misinterpret this. Let us recall when I was on that small river and was marked by a piece of the Sun itself, which entered into my left ankle. Since then until now, they have been trying to hinder me, as well as you, from coming to the famed and great prophet. But, as we can see, no one has succeeded, nor will they ever do so.

One evening when I lay down, my dears, I was unable to sleep for the entire night. As soon as I dozed off, I awoke, hearing the telephone ringing, voices, and seeing that sign opening in the Heavens, which more or less all recognize. On it, with it, and through this sign, I saw a river. It was exactly that river, the place where I received the piece of the Sun in my left ankle, and there I saw myself taking four rings, and the Voice said to me:

—You see, you have taken four seasons. Spring, fall, winter and summer.

I then came directly to a table and on this table stood a book, a tremendously great book. A woman sat there and this woman was connected to all the colors of the rainbow, that very rainbow you see after the rain. Then, she began to talk to me.

—Here is our prophet, his book is here.

The size of this book was such that I am not able to describe or explain it.

—Here you see; this is the book of life. For now you can openly say that you are a prophet and nothing more. I was transferred far away from my mother. I am the daughter, once Earth, now Atlantis. One child has already come to you, and another is on his way. My son, accept Pero, he has been sent to you also. All of those who come to you, this is how you will recognize them, and in a short while you will recognize them in a different way. When you write this book, say that Heaven is helping you.

And now, watch and observe, and you will see how a man with two people is crossing over that little river. It was then that another woman joined another table, and this was on the meadow. Please, she stood and said:

—This one is so and so, clear him.

I asked:

—And what is all this?

She answered me:

—You see that river? That is the small river where you received the four rings. Whoever passes over this place may never return. It is between death and life. It is the river of life. This river, it flows, you are always in that river. It is from there that you receive so much strength and so much energy. This is why you are the chosen one; it is on this river, the river of life, that you received the piece of the Sun, which entered into you. Many children were then marked. One is full of greed for money, another has been pushed into the underground world, but it is only you who has come out and you may never be hurt on this path. You are protected by the Heavens.

I asked:

—But this young man, he no longer returns to his children?

She said:

—No.

I said:

—But, I might bring him back.

To this she answered:

—You will be able to, but not now. You will be the only one to return to the bridge and enter through your own time, in your own time. These are the books of life, here is the river of life, this

is where all is written down, and these people who come to you in order to loyally and faithfully be in your service, these are all of your lives. So the time comes when you will be able to do anything, and everything that you say will make people happy. In this book of life, you will always find both yourself, as well as others.

Please, that young man had been taken away. In a short while, another big group of people arrived, and I watched them, but they did not see me.

I asked:

—How come they cannot see me?

She said to me:

—Your candle is connected, it burns; you are the light. You are still an earthly being. You can return back. The Heavens guard you, and this is why no one can harm you.

One day you saw that blond man; he will appear soon to you, to serve and follow you loyally and faithfully. He comes to you from the Heavens.

He will be your left side.

For now he is the life of your life.

Now you see that water, it washes away all the sins. This is the mechanism, and it is where all these people are now being taken, for they are no longer earthly people. They are souls now and they need to bathe in that water for their former life to be erased.

Whoever has not managed to pay off his karmic debt on Earth returns.

It is easily possible for them to do so and then repay. They will again be reborn as an earthly human. Three of you have left. Out of these three, one crept into the jaws and he is now with the underworld ruler. The one who supposedly served you, you thought all the best of him, yet instinctively, you knew that he belonged to the underground world, and that you had to send him there. You did this very well. He was your last obstacle, which you had to resolve without our help.

Now, when our help arrives, you will truly transform all the suffering, pain and sorrow that you have been carrying into great prosperity. Everything will go smoothly. Thus, you will also manage to gather this much of the world around you and show the way to a better future. You are the chosen one and you have been marked with the cross you carry on your forehead. You are the chosen one, so turn around, and look at the people crying out for you. Do not ask yourself why me any longer. Out of all of them, you have been awarded and given. You have passed through ten human months, that is ten astral days, and then another 27. Now you are on this last day of suffering.

You must pass through it all, and then the underground world will no longer have any effect over you. For a short while your father will be able to take satisfaction in your problems, but as we can see, you will destroy him with great love.

You have indeed said and spoken about everything that will happen. It will all be so, because it is thus written here in the Heavens; how you announced the awakening, how you announced the golden time, how you announced all of this. You have been given all and you will know all.

Awakening will soon come directly from me. I am a planet, taken away into space, where you will be paying me a visit soon. All that is sent comes directly from us, you will receive it all in time, and later when you tell it all in your desirable book, we will provide you with the explanations. All that you see here, you have seen from one life to the other. You are going directly from the past into the future.

You are the only one who returns back to this bridge. Go, and may prosperity follow you.

At the great door, I have been announced. And, I am leading you to a beautiful tomorrow.

GOLD PROTECTS THE EARTH

How does gold protect the Earth?

Gold is love. For now, gold is like an undiscovered metal. Please, everyone hides it in safes, in the country and everywhere. Everyone is afraid to wear it and eat with it.

Yet, I have announced that the one and only weapon against evil is GOLD. I am a man like you. The gold protects and guards humanity, it protects the Earth and wherever there is gold, whenever you are in trouble, you awaken your spirit guide, you awaken yourself so none can bring any harm upon you.

Why does evil flee from gold?

Because it carries the reflection of the Sun and it binds, as a salve on a wound.

The underground world sent thieves who quickly became the lords of this gold. They have reigned over it and locked it into vaults. But, this is only brief, until the awakening occurs. When humanity realizes how they have been asleep, they will awaken to say that they were naive. Had they not been able to eat with a gold spoon? There were these moments and others, when they were unable to do so because the gold had been locked into the vaults. Meanwhile, money was released to allow people to buy weapons to feed upon and kill one another, as the metal that protects and guards them had been taken away.

In the underground world, they rub their hands together and say, foolish mankind, they kill themselves and have no time to think about what we have locked up and taken away from them.

Well, my dears, by reading this book and poring back over it, come to know your bond, and find for yourselves that you are in a deep sleep.

Gold is your protection.

This is the main and only weapon and it has been taken away from you. Love has been replaced with hatred. Gold has been replaced with money; you are given this worthless paper and when you buy something or pay, negative energy rules over you. Money and only money. Money has been the greatest evil since the dawn of time to the present day....

This humanity is asleep and will remain sleeping till judgment day; that is until the awakening.

When I was married 17 years ago, my wife and I were given gold jewelry as a wedding present. We kept this gold at home and would occasionally wear a necklace or a ring. However, one day we saw that the gold had disappeared. We thought that someone had broken into our house. But, no money was taken. That valuable paper remained, but the gold was taken.

If thieves had broken into the house, surely they would have also taken the money. So we searched the entire house, but the gold was nowhere to be found. Where did the gold go if there were no thieves in the house?

I can safely say that one person deliberately took the gold. If this had happened to someone else, if the gold went missing in their house, they would first have suspected a friend, a relative or a neighbor. They would themselves simply enter the jaws of the underground world, by suspecting and accusing innocent people.

I did not do this, but I explained it to myself in another way. The person who gave me the gold was connected to the underground world. I was to be used to attack innocent people.

This is a method by which injustices occur. I would have gotten into a dreadful situation. I was supposed to be one hundred percent incapacitated, for I did not have any gold with me. By a miracle, something else happened.

Something amazing happened.

When I lay down to sleep at night, I was wearing the only gold that I had left on my hand and around my neck. I wore a gold chain with a pendant and my wedding ring.

When I woke up in the morning, I saw my ring was shattered. You will say that this is impossible, but it is possible.

During the great struggle, the chain disappeared from my neck, torn off, and the ring was broken. When I saw this I was stunned.

As there is an eternal battle between Good and Evil, so did a great battle take place between me and Evil. After that, I was no longer wearing the chain around my neck, and since the ring was broken, I took it to a jeweler where damaged gold pieces are sold and left it there. So, I was disarmed in matter, but I was strengthened by Spirit at the time and pulled through.

If you ask me whether I ever found my chain.

I did!

It was on July 15, 1990, in the evening. Before I went to bed, a voice said to me:

    —Before you lie down, open up your pillow.

I opened it.

    —Look at what you will find in the pillow.

To my great surprise, I saw the chain, which has been in my pillow for several years, so close that I was lying on it. And, I was protected by it.

So, I advise everyone; wear gold.

It will protect and guard you, as much as you want it to or not, because gold is the source of life. Do not do evil to anyone and it will not be returned. Gold will protect you, but wear it faithfully and look after it as you do yourself.

This is your direct mirror and do not be afraid that someone will steal it from you. No, they will not. If it is earned and proudly placed to protect you, we wish you a lot of happiness. That is why Ivica wears lots and lots of gold, and I have shown why he is symbolized by gold; this is why I wear it and why I will continue to wear it.

And why you will wear it when the time comes.

I remain, as you would say, the Golden man.

I have announced the golden time, when we will eat with a golden spoon. This is how deeply gold is with us and in the world.

You can see for yourself how strong negative energy is, for it cleared away the gold, and let loose money to the people to buy weapons. The one and only weapon against evil is gold. The gold protects and guards humanity, it protects the Earth and wherever there is gold, whenever you are in trouble, you awaken your spirit guide, you awaken yourself and no one can bring any harm upon you.

Evil runs away from gold!

As you know, I am the first in the world to be so publically ornate with gold. I wear it and will continue to wear it.

Yes, the key to everything is this: You are finding yourselves, and I am guiding you. There you have it, Gold protects humanity.

Your Ivica loves you very much, and may gold continue to protect you, along with me.

PROSPERITY IN THE HOME

We have had enough of this all: enough of misery, enough of turbulent times, enough of wars, enough of betrayal, enough of exile, enough of sadness and pain. So we ask ourselves: God, give me a bit of prosperity, for when there is a little bit of happiness in me, indeed this is all forgotten and I can begin that brighter tomorrow.

You will ask me, how do I see prosperity and how does it come about? And I would say: Everything is written in Destiny.

Destiny is the creator of all of this and it is written; about happiness and misery, about good and evil, and that we are as far from happiness and misery as by a mere thread. When we are grieving, we cannot rejoice and celebrate.

So by this, when a person falls and is unable to see his way, nor any doors, or handles or a keyhole, then in time he starts imagining something beautiful.

Please, I have already written that everything is recorded in Destiny, and that it is Fate which always comes in a timely manner, sending some good fortune. Here some happiness is coming into just this kind of a house.

Happiness comes just as misery does.

Until recently, we have been watching a man in misery, in sorrow, and we see that nothing has gone his way. I will leave you out of this and instead I will offer myself as an example.

Please, as I have described through all my books, I was rejected everywhere. Everyone used me in their own way, from my parents to my friends; I was the outcast who was rejected, and I never even thought that I would escape out of these kinds of jaws.

Well, my dears, one day, slowly but surely, good fortune knocked on my door. But, this time I had to sacrifice a lot of things in order to be a direct medium between Heaven and Earth, for everything that arrives to be shared with you.

Well, you see, I took myself as a living example and showed you the path from great misery to great happiness.

You are my happiness as I am yours.

By your arrival, you have shown that you have come in pureness to me, both in soul and in heart, and so for you I shall leave the door ajar.

And together with me directly, you will enter a brighter tomorrow.

Instead of your misery, there will be prosperity.

I say this for you to better understand and comprehend me: Happiness is so far away and yet so close. And, it is always present here with us.

This is also how it is when a household is dying, when they have nothing to eat, and are grieving and suffering.

This is where Fate has locked the door and said: Let them pass through karmic debt.

And then, afterwards a time arrives; their son is to be married. And when this young bride comes, she will deliver so much happiness that this household will be overrun by joy, prosperity and happiness.

When you, who live in the country, see that your farmyard has been unlucky for years, and this farmyard of yours is constantly under some kind of misfortune, so here all that you should gain perishes. And, you do not tell someone until this point, and this someone is actually your Fate, who comes to tell you: I see that you are suffering, grieving and fighting. Your neighbor says, I have, but you do not, neighbor. So this person gives you a pig, and when this new life comes, prosperity arrives just as misery once did.

Please, do not later become selfish and arrogant. Do not, please. That happiness was given to you for a specific period of time which may last for a year, two years or three years. As your livestock pens fill, you become greedy, and you make a lot of money. And the same person who gave it to you, or another one comes, and tells you the same story as you told a few years ago; unless you pass it on, you should understand, then your good fortune will go away just as it came, because it was only meant for that time. Here no one will ever help you, for you have closed your own door permanently.

All that I have said, I now tell in this book; how happiness comes into a house in sorrow, when one has hit rock bottom, when you do not even see a small light, when one should begin something new, with new life.

And, with this I would tell you, let the new life begin for you.

If you were not helped and your life not fundamentally changed, you would not request my help. I can freely say that I am not all-powerful. Yes, I am a human being like you. It is only that I can see the past, present and future.

Yes, you will ask me, Mr. Prokić, how is it that I feel so at ease and pleasant when I am around you? It is simply another life in your life, for you have been brought by an invisible energy.

To such questions, I would further respond:

> —*These are the lives of your ancestors who have tried to bring you and lead you to where you should go.*

Please, do not look at me as a doctor, since I am not a doctor and I will never be one. Medicine has absolutely nothing to do with me. Doctors are people who have been given to study at universities, in order to help in the physical world, when people are in trouble I would call them Fates. That is to say, Fate saves and mitigates this past life of yours, which is indeed being brought to a minimum, as well as attending to other lives after you, beyond this life.

I would never, God forbid, say anything against medicine when you all know I have the gift of foresight, so I know where these people come from.

I wish to cite an example:

You know yourself that so many flowers and so much comes to Srebrnjak 1 that it is incredible. What would you think if I were to trade those flowers or sell them? Do you think they would come back the following day? No, they would not.

I share the flowers where they are needed, and some remain with me at home, as well as at Srebrnjak 1. The amount of food that I receive, as much I share with the people. You have also been given it, so let this be stated here in this book, as much as I share, so much I receive.

A long time ago, I heard the Voice:

—*Here, I give you all these pens, all the stock and all of this.*

I asked myself; what will I do with it?

I see today that these are blessings, and as I give prosperity to all of these people, it is rationally displayed that these people bring it back. And, I cannot eat it all, so I give it to everyone.

I share with my coworkers, and we always have plenty.

Everything is full and every day we share it. Please, try to understand me; here is this happiness for you that comes.

If you were selfish, just as if I would be selfish, well, would I have had all that I have had?

I have a big heart and you are around me like ants, like bees who fly towards their mother. Well then, let this be a proclamation for the more beautiful tomorrow.

I guide you through time, into time, into the future, with much prosperity and an abundance of love.

WHY I WEAR GOLD

People known and unknown often wonder; from where does he get so much energy?

Where do I get all of this from and where is it all leading?

I will answer you briefly and clearly:

—I receive the energy directly from the Sun.

About five years ago, the voice told me:

—Ivica, you have 75 grams of gold, and when you have a kilogram of gold, you will be a direct guide with the Sun.

Then, I told people what I had experienced. They insulted and maligned me, they laughed and called me names.

Who would ever give me a kilogram of gold and wherein would it serve me? I wear Gold, it is what you see and it is notable on me, an ordinary mortal.

And, do you not ask yourself what does this mean?

Gold is the only visible basis that separates me from the rest of the world.

I do not have a kilogram, but two and a half kilograms of gold on me. Were this not the case, because you do not know me differently, I would appear strange to you without that much gold.

I wear gold because it symbolizes light. It is the light that you cannot steal, that even the most cunning thief cannot steal. It has strengthened me, it shines and it brings you directly to my energy. And the energy is growing stronger and stronger every day.

This energy is made up of our deceased ancestors. This is it. It is sufficient for it to shine and to strengthen me.

Look, to soothe you:

When you bring me, for instance, a ring and then you do not see it on my hand, do not be distressed, because this ring will go to someone to wear. It will go where it is needed and where I shall bestow it. But woe to the one who sells the Gold that you gave to me, which I gave to another. These are great and severe curses on this Gold, and they are meant to bury that person and take him straight into the underground world.

The moment I give people like this your Gold; that you painstakingly earned to present to your Ivica Prokić which he gave to another, and this other person sells it off, then there is no salvation. This person is directly in the underground world.

When I present a gift, I first wish the person great prosperity, much love, much joy and may it always lead him to the light. And, blessed is the one to whom it is presented. He who sells it off betrays, for this is holy Gold, as I just said. Then I give a great curse and to all similar people. Therefore, be careful what you take from my hands.

When you come to me, for that which was God-given to me, you want me to give to you, and I do this free of charge. I have never asked any of you to pay me for my precious time spent with you.

When you come to me, have you not asked yourself whether I have my own family? Do I have a wife and children? Am I married to you or to my wife? Do I need to have spare time for myself?

For you come like a river.

To this day, I have rarely seen anyone leave behind a Mark or a Kuna on my desk. That book would be bought, which I also need to pay for, and people leave. Someone will take a part of my energy, without ever asking; how do I eat?

Please, I have never had a price nor will I ever have one. I am priceless in value. But as much as you give, so much you bear. Ask for yourself whether fifty people, in effect a few million, have caught onto the matter and left a Kuna, a Mark, a dollar or something on the table?

For now, I can count you on my fingers.

Well, you ask me where I get so much energy?

Where do I give from and from where do I receive.

Please, when you go to the market and when you go to your company, in your company or wherever you go, do you work for free?

—*No.* You will answer.

You wait to be paid by the one for whom you work. And God pays me. It is with great and overwhelming energy. I give it to you, but what do you give me?

Some praise me, others spit on me, the third lie, the fourth ridicules. Well there, this is my payment. And what will happen in the future, you will see.

I have returned the blind back their sight, the lame to walk again, the sick to be healed, a barren woman to give birth ... when the woman became pregnant and gave birth to a child, I was sent therein to where she thought fit. Why would she come to see me now, after birthing her offspring?

I have also experienced this, my dear ones!

On one occasion, a child was born with my help, a female child. And *Vikend* published a picture of me with that child. The world on its own passed by, and after two years I went to visit the home of those people, and I was not allowed to see the child. They said I would put a spell on the child, so now I could not see her. I pleaded and begged to see the child, but they would not allow it. The child somehow heard me and ran to me. I gave the child money, and the mother accepted the money, but would not let me hold the child in my arms.

Do you know what happened to that child? The child went blind, deaf and mute.

Well, let them protect her at present, and see now that she has been born, she is suffering. One day the child will come to me, the child knows that I am her spiritual father. I would give anything in this world to be able to help her. How this will be and how it will end, we will see. Here is how my energy comes and how many people do not respect it. When the great energy grew stronger, there were so many people coming that for me to do it all on my own was no longer sufficient.

So, the Voice said:

—Now people will come, to do all the things that you have been doing on your own, from making coffee, preparing lunch, letting people in the door and bringing order to Tuškanova Street.

That is why God sent people, and they came to be called: The Association. And every day it grows stronger.

Let us recall that vision, which has happened in reality. It was at the "Hotel I", when I saw those six chains, which wrapped about me, and the seventh one went straight to my heart, so that I could fly everywhere and to any place.

I did not understand this back then, not until January 19, 1990, when I saw and was told:

—Now you have 75 grams of gold; go and tell your teacher Nikola everything, and then you will be a direct guide with the Sun.

All I have known, since that distant year of 1957, when I was bathing in that small river and a piece of the Sun entered my left ankle, I can freely say to this day, it is all symbolized by the Sun. And as we can see in all of this, gold is crucial. As you know, and can see, I have on so much gold and I am indeed very much tied to this gold.

A while ago, I told the story of my experience in the village of my birth, when the people said they saw the golden man and stated that the prophecy had come true. They said there was something shining out of me, just as the Sun shines forth with its rays.

I give you the words so you may judge for yourself what the meaning is of the man of gold and what the meaning is of the golden man.

I know that when I approach a person and shake their hand, the clinking can be heard from all of the gold I am wearing. People say they feel so blissful and that all their pains disappear.

I give you the task to judge for yourself what this gold signifies and why it shines so much out of me.

You be the judge of it.

GOOD FORTUNE HAS WON

Well then, good fortune has won.

This is the best living example; serendipity, when good fortune occurs in misfortune. So, whenever negative energy takes control over a person, good will come in to prevail. I would like to draw your attention to what I am saying, good fortune in misfortune. You invoke misfortune yourself, and this is how good fortune comes all on its own. It comes to someone when it is absolutely necessary.

When you see someone drowning, do not push him. Help him; maybe you are the Fate who needs to save this person so he will not perish, so nothing happens to him. When you see that someone is happy, rejoice with him. Do not bring adversity to him and do not wish him misery, because you will drag this misfortune onto yourself. Misfortune, as I just said, comes as good fortune does. Consequently, when you see something going on in the neighbor's yard, do not revel in his misfortune, but grieve with him together, so that the chalice passes you by. Love one another and create love. This much I have to say about good fortune and misfortune.

With this book, we will learn a lot; that there are no coincidences, that the future is coming and that happiness always comes when a person is miserable. People are fed up with lies, injustice and wars.

I have told you, I was rejected and adversities have always been set out for me, but as you can see, despite it all, I have survived and led all of my misfortunes to prosperity. My book signifies a step forward. This is my life. I have done everything that you wanted. I am the author. This is mine, namely yours.

I give you all of my books for safekeeping and to rejoice with them. I will be with you and will appear in your books, that is in my books, and you will read them. I wish all of my readers much happiness, good fortune and lots of love. I have never to this day charged for my work nor will I ever charge in the future. And all I get, you give yourselves. Some succeed, to someone a child is born, somebody gets a job, and another heals, so herein is my payment.

And, my biggest compensation is when a faithful follower, my admirer, comes bearing a bouquet of flowers. Here, this is my reward and these are my days for which I live. For you and you for me.

WHEN I AM NO LONGER HERE

In the end, I wish to say that not everyone can be a prophet. Being a prophet is a truly important matter. Maybe I was embarrassed being called a prophet, perhaps it still bothers me today, but I have no other choice. I have to continue the path that I have been given, and work in the way that I have been given. People who possess spiritual power are very rare. Among the 2.65 billion people, there is only one prophet. Predicting is not their choice. This is God-given.

Therefore, such people are not allowed be selfish, adulterous, and are not allowed to transfuse their work into business. What they have been given, they must give to others by imparting good, and they are not allowed to charge for it. They are ceaselessly tempted, and even more. Where they are the weakest is where they are most vulnerable, and if it is necessary, they may be pardoned here. In other words, what they deem for themselves, they must also deem for all others.

For example, I will mention a case from September 3, 1990, when I had a vision in which I was told:

> *...today something difficult will fall on Zagreb. At 12:55 p.m., there will be an earthquake. Now go and tell the nice people and say not to worry because everything will be alright.*

At exactly 12:55 p.m., it happened. People were astonished and can attest to this even today. When I was given the sign, there were fifteen people around me, who had come seeking my help. They all waited to see what would happen. And then it occurred.

It was exactly as I had foreseen it. There was a rumble, and as I said, nothing terrible happened. Everyone was stunned. How could I know about it five hours beforehand?

And how could I know that an earthquake would strike Zagreb at exactly 12:55 p.m.?

I explained to them that it had been spoken to me for I received the signs directly from the Sun. Everything I have to say, I do not conceal anything, I tell all exactly as I see it and feel it.

When I could, I would always wish for only the good to happen. As we know, there are no coincidences because everything is predetermined, and so that which I see I have to relay. Whether it is bad or beautiful, I have to convey it exactly as I see it.

And, I saw a stout, balding man who told me:

—You, Ivica, will no longer give people inscriptions!

I felt sad and sorry. Then, he comforted me:

—This will no longer be necessary, for you shall be a direct guide with the Sun.

Then I was told that I would hand over all that I have done and all that I do to a young man and he would continue my work.

And, I will help in a different way.

Please Visit

USA Website: www.Braco.net
USA Webstore: www.BracoStore.com

European Website: www.Braco-info.com
European Webshop: www.Braco-Shop.com

Live Streaming: www.Braco-Europe.tv
Facebook: www.Facebook.com/Braco.Ivica